So much practical, down-to-earth wisdom within that you'll want to revisit time and time again: read this with a highlighter pen to hand!'

Amanda Alexander PCC, talent development
coach and regional director of Forward Ladies

'Grace's tips are the kind you can use in your own life and get real results.'

John Williams, author of Screw Work, Let's Play

'Full of practical suggestions, hints and tips to get the most out of your busy schedule.'

June Dennis, head of the University
of Wolverhampton business school

brilliant

productivity

PEARSON

At Pearson, we believe in learning – all kinds of learning for all kinds of people. Whether it's at home, in the classroom or in the workplace, learning is the key to improving our life chances.

That's why we're working with leading authors to bring you the latest thinking and best practices, so you can get better at the things that are important to you. You can learn on the page or on the move, and with content that's always crafted to help you understand quickly and apply what you've learned.

If you want to upgrade your personal skills or accelerate your career, become a more effective leader or more powerful communicator, discover new opportunities or simply find more inspiration, we can help you make progress in your work and life.

Pearson is the world's leading learning company. Our portfolio includes the Financial Times and our education business, Pearson International.

Every day our work helps learning flourish, and wherever learning flourishes, so do people.

To learn more, please visit us at **www.pearson.com/uk**

productivity

Grace Marshall

PEARSON

Harlow, England • London • New York • Boston • San Francisco • Toronto • Sydney • Auckland • Singapore • Hong Kong
Tokyo • Seoul • Taipei • New Delhi • Cape Town • São Paulo • Mexico City • Madrid • Amsterdam • Munich • Paris • Milan

PEARSON EDUCATION LIMITED
Edinburgh Gate
Harlow CM20 2JE
United Kingdom
Tel: +44 (0)1279 623623
Web: www.pearson.com/uk

First published 2016 (print and electronic)

ISBN: 978-1-292-08340-7 (print)
      978-1-292-08342-1 (PDF)
      978-1-292-08341-4 (ePub)

British Library Cataloguing-in-Publication Data
A catalogue record for this book is available from the British Library

Library of Congress Cataloging-in-Publication Data
Names: Marshall, Grace (Productivity coach), author.
Title: Brilliant productivity / Grace Marshall.
Description: Harlow, England : Pearson Education, 2016. | Includes index.
Identifiers: LCCN 2015038010 | ISBN 9781292083407
Subjects: LCSH: Time management. | Performance. | Mental efficiency.
Classification: LCC HD69.T54 M379 2016 | DDC 650.1—dc23
LC record available at http://lccn.loc.gov/2015038010

10 9 8 7 6 5 4 3 2 1
19 18 17 16 15

Series cover design by David
Print edition typeset in 10/14
Print edition printed in the U

NOTE THAT ANY PAGE CR(

To Grante, Oliver and Catherine, who inspire me to be good enough, most of the time, with intermittent lapses into hopelessness and brilliance.

Contents

About the author

Grace Marshall is head coach and chief encourager at Grace-Marshall.com, author of *21 Ways to Manage the Stuff That Sucks Up Your Time* and a Productivity Ninja with Think Productive, one of the world's leading productivity training companies.

Grace admits she's not a naturally organised person. Her passion for productivity began when she got fed up of saying 'I haven't got enough time'.

She believes in changing the world, one conversation at a time – whether that's on stage, in the workshop room, with coaching clients, over a cuppa, on the page or on screen. You can start a conversation with her on Twitter @GraceMarshall or email grace@grace-marshall.com

She lives in Stafford with her husband and their two children. When she's not working (and sometimes when she is), you'll probably find her surrounded by people, books, music, board games, faith and food – possibly even all at once.

Acknowledgements

All good things start with a conversation.

So my first thanks go to Graham Allcott at Think Productive and Steve Temblett at Pearson, for the conversation that started this book, and to Amanda Alexander for the conversations that kept me sane while writing it.

Special thanks also to Caroline, Eve, Fokke, Jacob, Jennie, Jenny x3, Jim, Josie, June, Katy, Marianne, Penny, Rebekah, Richard, Rob, Ruth, Sian, Susie and Wendy for the conversations that helped to shape this book.

Most of all to my clients, readers, workshop and conference delegates I get the privilege to work with – your questions keep me writing. Keep them coming . . .

Publisher's acknowledgements

We are grateful to the following for permission to reproduce copyright material:

Figure on page 207 after *The 7 Habits of Highly Effective People*, Simon & Schuster (Stephen R. Covey, 2005).

CHAPTER 1

How productive are you?

What is personal productivity?

Depending on who you ask, you'll probably get different answers. Your first thoughts might be along the lines of:

- ticking things off a to-do list
- getting work done in the time that you have
- meeting deadlines
- setting goals and achieving them.

If we dug a little deeper, it might also be about:

- feeling in control/on top of your workload
- doing meaningful work
- making progress, seeing results
- enjoying a sense of 'job done' satisfaction
- knowing what you do matters
- 'finding time' for what matters
- not letting people down
- having a life outside of work.

And if I asked you what *doesn't* feel productive, this is often where the picture becomes even clearer:

- running round like a headless chicken
- a to-do list that grows quicker than you can tick things off
- being busy all day and wondering what you've actually accomplished

- running out of time
- missing important deadlines – at work and in personal life
- feeling stuck, waiting for someone or something else before you can make progress
- wasting time
- doing pointless work
- being unclear about what you need to do – or what you have done
- feeling guilty about what you haven't done
- always feeling like there isn't enough time.

What makes a day productive isn't just the number of tasks you tick off a to-do list. It's the satisfaction, the sense of achievement and progress, and the knowledge that what you do matters. It's waking up looking forward to doing your best work and having fun doing it. It's coming home feeling satisfied and enjoying life outside of work. It's about experience as well as achievement. It's about the quality of your life at work as well as the work itself.

What's the difference between time spent and time well spent? Between brilliant productivity and just getting things done? Yes, it's satisfying to tick things off a list. Yes, there are days when just surviving is a rewarding achievement. But over the longer term, it's not enough to just go through the motions. You need meaning, purpose and joy.

Meaning

Does what you're doing matter? More importantly, does it matter to you? We all need to know that what we're doing matters. That we're not just cranking some big hamster wheel, churning out stuff for the sake of it. Time only feels productive when what you spend it on is personally meaningful.

Purpose

Purpose gives you direction and drive. It distinguishes between activity and action, from going through the motions to actually making progress. It's what makes the difference between dragging yourself out of bed to work, and tearing yourself away from it (and remembering to eat and sleep). When you know you are contributing to something bigger than yourself, purpose gives you the determination to go beyond your comfort zone and the resilience to press through the tough times. Purpose calls the best out of us, and gives us the deepest satisfaction from our work.

Joy

What is productivity without joy? Without joy, work becomes empty drudgery and an interminable chore. As human beings we are designed to derive joy from working – to feel good about putting our effort into something and seeing it grow into something more. There is something incredibly soul satisfying about getting to the end of the day and feeling what can only be described as 'good knackered'– when you are naturally tired but incredibly alive. When you enjoy the work – and the times when you're not working – as well as the fruits of your labour.

What's your personal definition of productivity?

Think about the last time you got to the end of a day that felt truly productive.

- What kind of work were you doing?
- What did you enjoy most about it?
- What wider purpose did it fulfil?
- What made it personally meaningful?
- How often do you experience this? What would it be like to experience it on a much more regular basis?

brilliant action

My personal definition of productivity is:

....

....

How productive are you?

True productivity is satisfaction in a world where the work never ends. Excitement without exhaustion. Opportunity without overwhelm. It is the ability to give our best in any situation, and to keep giving our best. To be on fire with passion and purpose, without burning out. To work, rest and play, without feeling guilty. To enjoy the crazy times without going crazy, and the calm times without getting bored.

And there are eight arenas in which this plays out.

Managing your work

Productivity is about doing the work, rather than letting the work do you. It's about managing the incoming and the ongoing, the urgent tasks and the long-term projects, the emails, the meetings, the colleagues and your own ideas. Achieving clarity and a sense of 'job done' satisfaction in a world where work never ends.

How 'on top' of your workflow are you currently?

Managing yourself

Your thoughts, feelings, habits and resistance – the way you think – can create motivation, focus and momentum that enable your productivity, or they can create procrastination, fear and resistance that shuts everything down. The more you understand what's going on inside your head, the more you can harness your best thinking, rather than fight your inner mind monkeys.

How often do you find yourself procrastinating?

Prioritising 'best' over 'busy'

Being busy isn't hard. There is always work to do, but being too busy can stop you from doing your best work. True productivity is about distinguishing between the fake work that just keeps you busy, from the real work that produces real results.

How much of your daily work is actually productive action that produces real results?

How you work with others

None of us work in a bubble. Our ability to work productively depends on how we work with others – how we communicate and collaborate instead of distract and disrupt each other. How we work with other people's priorities, schedules and tendencies, as well as manage expectations, delays and last-minute emergencies.

How well do you work with your clients and your colleagues? How much do you help or hinder each other's productivity?

Managing boundaries

When we try and please everybody all of the time, we end up stretching ourselves thin and diluting our resources. To do our best work, we need to be able to say no, to establish boundaries and expectations that enable us to give our best.

Do you have healthy boundaries in place? Are you clear about what you say no to?

Working with your personality (not against it)

Productivity is personal. There is no one-size-fits-all solution. Your best productivity strategies are ones that are tailored to your personality and harness your strengths, rather than fight, dismiss or suppress it.

How clear are you about your *personal* productivity strategies?

Sustaining momentum

Productivity isn't just about how you create momentum, it's also about how you sustain, recover and recharge that momentum. It's about fuel, rhythm and balance. It's about how you get started, keep going and keep on keeping on.

How sustainable is your productivity right now? Are you close to burnout, or do you have sustainable momentum?

Overcoming overwhelm

Overwhelm, stress and guilt are commonplace in today's world of work, but if left unchecked, they can kill your productivity. How you respond to these feelings can make the difference between doing your best work, and never doing enough.

How much does stress, overwhelm and guilt currently feature in your work and life?

Work in progress

Productivity is a work in progress. There is no such thing as perfection. This book will give you plenty of practical guidance, tools and techniques, as well as opportunities and insights to reflect on what's working, and what can work better.

Don't use it as a stick to beat yourself up, a prescription to follow blindly, or an idealised view of perfection to highlight all the areas where you don't measure up.

Do use it as a tool to identify and inspire change. Use it as insight that shines a light on what you're doing well and what's getting in your way (not what's wrong with you). Use it as a menu – not everything to be consumed at once, but a selection of tips and techniques to taste and digest, as and when you have the appetite. Use it as a personal tool, to enable you to do your best work, to inspire your best ideas and to unlock your brilliance. Above all, have fun using it, because after all, that's what brilliant productivity is ultimately about – doing your best work, having fun doing it, and enjoying life at work and life outside of work.

CHAPTER 2

Organising your work

Productivity isn't just about how fast or how much you work. It's about managing your work and the way that you work, so that you are able to focus your attention on the right things at the right time, and feel like you're on top of your workflow, rather than drowning in it.

This chapter will give you tips and strategies to manage your projects, actions, ideas and nags – to keep track of things that are pending or waiting, to have a bird's eye view of 'everything' on your plate, as well as laser focus when you need to get that next critical task done. It will show you how to regularly have 'job done' satisfaction in a world where work never ends, and how to manage your working environment and identify what really steals your time.

Managing workflow

What makes today's world of work particularly chaotic?

1 **The work never ends.** The days come and go, but there is always more to be done. More calls you can make, more research you can do, more errands to run, ideas to pursue, people to connect with, leads to follow up on, more emails that land in your inbox, more requests, more opportunities, more horizons to explore, more challenges to meet, more targets to break . . .

2 **Work doesn't form an orderly queue.** Work arrives at different times, in different ways and progresses at

different speeds. Our job is not just to do the work. It's to work out the work – to define the work, to choose the work, to manage the work, to juggle the work . . .

3   **Life doesn't stop when you work.** Of course, it's not just the work. It's the life outside of work – from everyday chores like taking out the bin and buying toothpaste, to things you keep meaning to get round to, like making that doctor's appointment, calling your mother or writing your will, to big things like moving house, getting married and choosing high schools, and fun things, like seeing friends, building kit cars, band practice, marathon training or going on holiday – and even simple things like eating and sleeping! All this needs to happen too, in between, around and alongside the work.

Sometimes it feels like everything's moving in different directions, waiting for a spectacular crash. Other times it's gridlock. Nothing's moving. There's traffic, there's noise, it's stressful but nothing seems to be moving forward.

That's when we need some traffic control.

Traffic control

Managing workflow is a bit like traffic control. If you let everything run in every direction, there's chaos. Nothing gets done, everything goes crazy and you're likely to see some spectacular crashes.

Think of all the things you have on your plate right now – tasks, projects, errands, chores, ideas, nags, reminders – at work, at home, in your personal life, your social life . . .

How many things do you have on your to-do list and on your radar right now? How much of it is on 'red', where you're stuck and don't know how to move forward. How much is on amber, where you're waiting for someone else, something else or even on your decision before you can move forward? How much is on green, where you're good to go?

Red – what's stuck?

What's stuck but still on your radar? Maybe you've hit a dead end. Maybe it's not quite worked out how you thought it would. Maybe a supplier has just pulled out of a deal at the last minute, or a company restructure has thrown a spanner in the works. Maybe you're stuck and haven't figured out the next step, or maybe it's completely dead but still on your radar: abandoned but still on the road; done but not quite dusted. What's been hanging around for way too long, gathering dust on your to-do list?

When we have too many things on red, we feel frustrated. Nothing's moving forward, everything's stuck: we need to figure out a way forward. When we have a few things on red – but stuck permanently there – it might be tempting to ignore them, and let the 'green' traffic work its way around them. But that still takes up space on the road, and makes it harder work for the traffic to flow.

↗ brilliant reflection

- What do you need to release? To take off the road completely?
- What do you need to take action on to get unstuck?
- What do you need help with?

Amber – what's on hold?

What's pending on your to-do list? What are you waiting on someone else for? What will you get round to 'some day'?

That piece of information you're waiting on, the lead time you need to give someone else to make a decision, the time it takes for an order to be processed or a decision to be authorised, the work you've delegated, decisions you're delaying . . .

Whether you've chosen to put that piece of work on pending, or you're waiting for someone else to come back to you, revving your engines at an amber light, poised to take action but not actually going anywhere, takes effort, energy and distracts you from the work that you can be getting on with.

What do you need to park instead?

@Waiting – for the things you're waiting on
Waiting for Joe from accounts to send you those figures before you can do anything else with your presentation? Tracking a missing parcel and need to wait seven days before you can chase? Want to set yourself a reminder to follow up a sales enquiry if you haven't heard back in the next two weeks?

Instead of carrying it around in your head, keep track of these things in a 'waiting for' list, or an @waiting category on your to-do list, where you can check in regularly and nudge or chase when you need to. Keep this separate from your 'actions', the things that you can be working on right now, so that you don't create a stop–start momentum where you keep bouncing between 'Yes I can do that: go go go' and 'No I can't do that right now, still waiting: stand down'.

brilliant tip

Instead of having a giant to-do list, separate your tasks into categories and assign an @ tag to make it easy to find. So when you want to find all the things you're waiting for, you can search for @waiting. If you want to find all the things that you need to talk to your boss about, you can search for @boss.

Ideas park – for the things you choose to put off

When you have an idea for a blog post, an interesting new tool you've discovered, campaigns you might want to run in future, a project that's on the back burner, a book to add to the reading list, that brilliant shiny new idea you've just had when you were trying to focus – that's when an ideas park comes in handy.

An ideas park is somewhere where you can physically store an idea, out of your head so it stops distracting you, and keep it safe for you to come back to when you're ready to actually do something with it. You could use a separate notebook, the back pages of your notebook, a physical or electronic file, a tag or category on your to-do list app, or even keep an actual ideas jar on your desk:

---

brilliant example

Sarah finds that her best ideas always come when she is trying to focus on something else. Instead of trying to ignore them, store them in her head, or chase each tangent as it arrives, she keeps an ideas jar on her desk. Every time she has an idea that's different to what she's focusing on, she writes it down on a piece of paper, folds it up and puts it in the jar. That way she gets it out of her head, and keeps it safe, and her ideas jar becomes like a treasure chest, full of ideas to explore when she's ready.

Green – what's good to go?

So everything should be green right? Well, not quite. Giving everything the green light creates exactly the kind of chaos you would imagine if all the traffic lights at a busy junction suddenly turned green. You have havoc, cars cutting up left right and centre, some spectacular crashes and near misses, lots of swerving and eventually gridlock . . . it would be total chaos.

We can do anything but not everything at once. Our productivity depends as much on how well we manage the traffic as how well we drive the car (do the work). And when we manage it well, the traffic flows, and driving becomes a dream, rather than a danger.

Managing the incoming

How do you manage the incoming stuff? Do you just tend to react to whoever's shouting the loudest, or what happens to land in your inbox when you're looking? Do you deal with things as soon as they arrive, or do you let it all pile up and see which one floats to the top? Do you catch everything that arrives, or do some fall through the cracks? Or do you duck and hide and hope nothing sticks?

If there's always more work to be done (and arguably more work than can be done) dealing directly with the incoming is exhausting, unrewarding and can lead to perpetual firefighting and constantly reacting to whatever's shouting the loudest, rather than progressing the things that matter to you, that perhaps nobody else would chase you for. But not dealing with the incoming can also lead to being bogged down by backlogs, missing things, forgetting, and a constant sense of playing catch up and not quite knowing what you've overlooked that might come back to bite you.

The CORD Productivity Model

The Think Productive CORD Productivity Model is a useful way to help you think about how you manage everything you need to get done in work (and life).[1]

CORD stands for Capture and Collect, Organise, Review and Do.

Capture and Collect

Firstly, think about everything you need to capture and collect: actions, ideas, tasks, projects, things you're waiting on others for. Where do you capture this information? In a notebook or several notebooks, in your inbox, on a scrap of paper, straight onto your to-do list or do you try and keep it all in your head? How robust are these capture and collect points? How easy, accessible and simple are they to use? Does anything ever fall through the cracks?

Organise

Organise is about defining the work. The job here is to filter from a mass of ideas to 'what's worth doing?' and 'what's the next action?' This part of traffic control is about parking what's pending or waiting, deleting what's not worth doing, and making sure what goes on the road is fit for purpose, i.e. well defined, specific next actions.

Review

Review is where you go fully into boss mode and check in with the bigger picture. It's the time to stop 'doing' and think about everything you've got on your plate. How is everything going? What's on track? What's next? This is where you review your projects and make decisions about direction and priority. What do you need to make space for this week? What's your focus? It's also a good time to check in with yourself: how are you feeling? What are you resisting? How's your energy? Are you making time for what's important to you? What do you need to do differently?

Do

Do is about ruthless execution and effortless momentum. Having captured, defined and reviewed the work, this is the time to get on and do. Drive the car. Focus on the road ahead.

Make the journey. Get the job done. Even then, there are things that can get in the way – distractions, obstacles, bumps in the road, unexpected road closures and U-turns. Things you need to respond and react to in the moment – but with less of the reactive in your day to day, you'll find you are more prepped and primed to respond in the moment.

↗ brilliant reflection

How much time do you spend in each of these modes of working? Do you go straight from Capture to Do mode, instead of taking the time to Organise and Review the work? Or do you spend all your time Organising and Reviewing, then stalling when it comes to the Doing? How strong is your CORD?

Done

Technically this is part of the Do stage – or the result of the Do stage of the CORD Productivity Model, but it's something that so often gets overlooked, I think it's worth a mention here.

Done. Actually ticking it off the list, closing it off and celebrating that achievement before moving on. We often miss out on this stage because we're so busy moving onto the next one, but here's why it's important. It's about switching off. It's about actually finishing – doing that very last step that marks the project complete, instead of letting it hang around as that tiny thing you just have to do.

It may be where you're tempted to keep tweaking, instead of publishing and sending it out there. Or it may be where you get bored, and stop slightly short of the finish line. Either way, you keep it in motion. It's still part of the traffic you're managing, still taking up space on the road, still requiring a little bit of your attention.

Maybe that last thing is actually just filing it away, deleting the email or archiving the project. There's nothing left to be done but it's still taking up space and you're still having to navigate around it.

'in place' vs 'in use'

Kitchen designers and professional organisers both work on the principle of 'dynamic order', the idea that things don't stay in one place all the time, but everything needs a place to be 'in use' and to be 'in place' when it is not in use. For example, when kids are playing, toys are 'in use' and belong on the floor. It can look like a mess but the toys are exactly where they're supposed to be. When they've finished playing, that's when the toys need to be tidied away, and go back 'in place'.

Clutter happens when you leave things 'in use', instead of putting them back 'in place'. The letters you read but don't action. The paperwork you leave on the side because you still need to do something with it. Tasks and projects you have on the go and haven't mentally put down. Things you don't need any more but haven't let go of. Things you do need to keep, but haven't quite decided where they go.

I see the same thing happen with emails in the 'Getting your inbox to zero' workshops I run. Inboxes start as a place for incoming items, then typically become a dumping ground for emails that:

- need to be actioned
- don't need to be actioned
- need to be read
- have been read but still need figuring out
- are waiting on someone else's action

- are waiting on your decision
- have been actioned (but not quite got round to filing away).

Do you have too many things 'in use'?

When we have too many things 'in use' we don't use any of them properly. Everything gets in the way and nothing gets enough focus. We just end up paper shuffling, wading through the mess and yelping when we stand on Lego. Moving things around rather than using them. Being surrounded by toys rather than playing with them. Being surrounded by work rather than actually working.

Putting things back 'in place' – whether that's a physical place or mentally switching off – can help us to focus on the things that do need our attention. The actions, the work, the things we need to 'do'.

It's also about momentum and motivation. The satisfaction of getting things done. When we stop to acknowledge our progress, it gives us fuel to do more. It reminds us what we're capable of.

Celebrating success

What we focus on grows. Research suggests we actually have three times more positive experiences than negative, but two main tendencies keep us from experiencing, extending, and expanding our joy: the negativity bias – that our minds have a natural tendency to linger on and give more weight to negative experiences – and habituation – when things become so familiar that they lose their power to amaze and captivate us.[2]

One way to counter this is to deliberately focus on what's going well. To intentionally savour and relive the positive experiences by writing them down, capturing them and sharing them.

brilliant tip

Celebrate what you want to see more of. Experiment with making a daily 'ta-da list' or use a service like **idonethis.com** to keep track of your achievements, your celebrations, gratitude and blessings.

And don't just keep it to yourself, share it with someone who cares. Research has found that 'discussing positive experiences leads to heightened wellbeing, increased overall life satisfaction and even more energy . . . sharing our joy increases joy. Telling people about our happiness has far greater benefits than just remembering it or writing it down for ourselves'.[3] It turns out this increases the wellbeing of those around us too. That joy can be contagious, or as Nobel Peace Prize winner Albert Schweitzer said: 'Happiness is the only thing that multiplies when you share it.'

Here are some simple ways you can practise celebrating success:

- Keep a daily journal, gratitude list or 'ta-da' list.
- Share your daily, weekly or monthly wins with a coach, mentor or friend.
- Start each team meeting with 'what's your good news?' (or make it part of your dinner table conversation).
- Have a celebrations board in your office.
- Set up a 'champagne moments' folder in your email to store testimonials, positive feedback and thank you emails.
- Use a service like idonethis.com to keep track of your daily wins.

Managing your work environment

With open offices and open communication channels on the go 24/7, it's easy to find yourself being continually interrupted and distracted. A study of Microsoft workers found that when working on something that required a significant level of focus, it took an average of 15 minutes to recover attention from a one-minute interruption.

One minute to take that call, check that email, answer that colleague's question. Fifteen minutes to recover your attention, remember where you were up to, reread the last paragraph, get back into the flow of what you were doing before.

Ever get to the end of the day when you're closing down your computer and you find that email you started to write at 9 am?

Recent research from Middle Tennessee State University also found that being distracted by personal social media leads to negative effects on efficiency and wellbeing. Participants were asked to watch a 15-minute video on a computer, with tabs left open for a number of social media sites, including Facebook, Twitter and LinkedIn. They were monitored to see how often they checked social media, and were tested on the video's content. Those who used the sites more did not perform as well as those who used them less – and were also found to have 'higher levels of technostress and lower happiness'.[4]

How many times do you get interrupted in your working day? How often are you distracted by what else is going on in your world, in your head or on your desktop? How much of your attention is that stealing?

Common sources of distraction include:

- colleagues in the office
- phone calls
- emails
- your boss
- instant messaging chat
- social media
- the report that's still sitting on your desk from last week

- background noise
- you! Thoughts of other work, nags, reminders, new ideas . . .

What about sensory noise?

Our senses gather some 11 million bits per second from our environment – but our conscious mind can only process about 50 bits per second. We all filter out information, but some people are more sensitive to certain noise than others.

brilliant example

My husband works best in total silence. He's particularly sensitive to noise that comes from people - chatter and crowds. Blocking out background noise takes up a certain amount of effort and energy, so even when he can filter out the noise, he doesn't have his full attention to pay to the work at hand. He notices that noise also creeps up on him. He may not notice it building up, until all of a sudden it's completely unbearable.

In contrast, I don't work too well in a totally quiet or static environment. I find that background noise and movement stimulates me and gets my brain working better than in complete silence. The only exception is when I'm on a phone call or a webinar – when what I need to focus on is auditory. Otherwise, give me the hum-drum of a café, with people coming and going, background chatter and music I can hum to any day. In fact, that's where most of this book has been written - in the corner of a wonderful little local café that serves amazing aubergine caponata.

brilliant reflection

What's your optimal working environment? And how well is your current environment working for you? Does it stimulate you, over-stimulate you or bore you? Does it get your creative juices flowing or overload your senses? Does it wake your brain up or shut it down?

Noise control

If you find your environment is too much on the noisy side (or has the wrong kind of noise) here are some ways you can turn it down.

Reducing digital noise

- Turn off email notifications.
- Turn off social media notifications.
- Unsubscribe from newsletters or notifications you no longer need.
- Set up a rule to filter out the things that you want to pay less attention to into a circulars or read later folder.
- Put chat programs to offline/unavailable for the times when you don't want to talk.
- Turn off automatic send/receive (or go into work offline mode on your email).
- Turn off the wifi.
- Don't leave email open in the background (same goes for social media).
- Close tabs/windows when you're finished before moving onto the next thing.

Reducing physical noise

- Use headphones.
- Close the door.
- Change location: work from home/meeting room/café.
- Have an agreed 'do not disturb' signal in open offices.
- Communicate your availability (more on this in Chapter 5).
- Clear clutter from your desk.

Reducing noise in your own head

- Write it down, get it out of your head.
- Use a trusted 'second brain' system to capture ideas, reminders and nags.
- Focus on one thing at a time, stop trying to multitask.
- Give yourself a visual reminder of the thing you're working on (e.g. Post-it note).
- Calm your mind monkeys (more on this in Chapter 3).

A note about multitasking

Multitasking: some people love it, some hate it. Some see it as necessity when juggling multiple roles, responsibilities, commitments and projects. But does it actually work?

Multitasking isn't actually multitasking. What we perceive to be multitasking is actually rapidly refocusing between tasks. While it might feel productive, each switch costs you time, attention and productivity – sometimes just a few tenths of a second, sometimes much more (remember the Microsoft experiment? 1 minute interruption = average 15 minute recovery) especially when you're repeatedly switching back and forth between tasks. Research suggests that even brief mental blocks created by shifting between tasks can cost as much as 40 per cent of your productive time.[5]

---

brilliant example

Spotted on Twitter: 'I feel like I have too many tabs open in my head!'

Do you ever feel like that? What happens when you have too many tabs open on your computer? It slows down, crashes, or stops working. It's also ▶

easier to get distracted when clicking between tabs – to accidentally click on the wrong tab, or let something shiny catch your eye, and end up going off on a tangent. Have you ever been closing down your tabs and windows at the end of the day, only to find that one email you forgot to press send on first thing in the morning?

It's much easier to make mistakes when multitasking. Have you ever sent the email to the wrong person? Or worse, sent it to the person you were talking about rather than the person you wanted to talk to?

If you came to my house at breakfast time, you might argue that multitasking is a necessity, but believe me it doesn't take much – one spilt drink, one squabble, one child suddenly remembering they're supposed to be wearing something blue that day – for me to burn the toast or put the dishwasher tablet in the coffee. So yes, sometimes the world doesn't form an orderly queue to wait for our full attention and we do have to juggle multiple tasks from time to time, but be aware that when your attention is split, nothing is getting your full and best attention. Give yourself a break and don't throw in any more balls to juggle than you have to.

Is there ever a good time to multitask?

There are times when splitting your attention can be quite useful. If you're running, you might like to listen to a podcast to actively take your mind off the ache in your legs.

Other ways of 'killing two birds with one stone' could include:

- walking meetings
- car sharing or travelling to an event with a colleague you want to catch up with
- listening to audio books while commuting

- watching a video while on the treadmill (*only* on a treadmill, this does not work on the road!)

- taking your ideas into the bath – and keeping bath crayons or a diver's slate handy to capture any bright ideas.

 **recap**

The bad news is, the work never ends. The good news is, productivity is not about getting to the end of all the work. It's simply about managing your workflow, your environment and your attention in a way that allows you to focus your attention on the right things at the right time, and feel like you're on top of your workflow, rather than drowning in it.

With some good traffic control and a strong CORD in place, you can manage your workflow, even when you have multiple roles and projects, and competing commitments and deadlines. You can create momentum that allows your best work to flow, and celebrate 'job done' success and satisfaction on a regular basis.

References

[1] Allcott, G., 2014. *How to be a Productivity Ninja: Worry Less, Achieve More and Love What You Do.* Icon Books: London.

[2] Psychology Today, 2013. 'The science behind the joy of sharing joy'. Available at: www.psychologytoday.com/blog/feeling-it/201307/the-science-behind-the-joy-sharing-joy

[3] Ibid.

[4] Brooks, S., 2015. 'Does personal social media usage affect efficiency and well-being?' *Computers in Human Behavior* (Volume 46). Available at: http://www.sciencedirect.com/science/article/pii/S0747563215000096

[5] American Psychological Association, 2010. 'Stress in America findings'. Available at: www.apa.org/news/press/release/stress/2010/national-report.pdf

CHAPTER 3

Thinking productively

Distractions and procrastination have far more impact on your productivity than your time management skills. This chapter will show you how to identify and understand the 'inner stuff' that hampers your productivity, and provides practical tools and strategies to help deal with and overcome these hurdles.

Understanding your brain

Why do we leave things to the last minute – and then freak out at the deadline? Why when we need courage do we scare ourselves more? Why do we insist on winding ourselves up with disaster thinking? Why do we say we want one thing, then do the complete opposite?

The answer is this. We have monkeys living in our brain.

In his book *The Chimp Paradox*, Professor Steve Peters describes three different parts to the human brain:[1]

1 The Human Brain – which makes logical, purposeful decisions, motivated by fulfilment, self-development, morals and ethics.

2 The Chimp Brain – which is responsible for survival, driven by primitive emotional drives such as fear, ego and rage (and yes, the reproductive drive). It is extremely risk averse and sees all change as potential danger. It will protect you from being in the limelight, being visible,

bucking the trend, doing something new, taking risks, making changes – because what it doesn't know it can't control, and what it can't control it can't stop from hurting you.

3 The Computer Brain – automatic habits which can be operated by the human or the chimp . . .

Seth Godin refers to the chimp brain as the lizard brain: 'Want to know why so many companies can't keep up with Apple? It's because they compromise, have meetings, work to fit in, fear the critics and generally work to appease the lizard . . . The amygdala isn't going away. Your lizard brain is here to stay, and your job is to figure out how to quiet it and ignore it.'[2]

Other people refer to their mind monkeys – sometimes there's just one, sometimes it feels like there's a whole gang of them chattering away in there! Whether you see it as your mind monkey, your lizard brain or your inner critic, there's definitely something that goes on inside our heads, that creates resistance, generates fear, tempts us to procrastinate, and drives us to distraction.

What's going on in your head? And what can you do about it? Let's take a deeper look shall we?

Understanding your mind monkeys

Here are six tactics that our mind monkeys often use. Which ones do you recognise?

1. Distract you

Your monkey gets bored easily. It likes to play. Faced with the spreadsheet that bores you to death, your monkey sees it as his mission to find you something much more interesting to do. Faced with a big problem to solve, something difficult or scary, your monkey finds a million things that would take your mind off it.

Essentially your monkey just wants everyone to get along and have fun, so when it sees you struggling with something, it helpfully offers you some light relief. Except your monkey is also extremely short-sighted and has the attention span of a three-year-old. It can't see that the struggle will only get worse if you keep leaving it, or that eventually you'll have to hand in that piece of work anyway and feel bad about the poor job you did, or that beyond the struggle is a whole heap of fun if you can just get this boring bit done first.

2. Beat you up

Remember how excited you were when you first had that idea? Or the motivation you had when you bounced out of that conference? Or even the last award you won when you *knew* that it was all worthwhile, that finally here was proof that you *can* do it.

This heavy-hitting monkey still comes back with the same message: you're not good enough/clever enough/fast enough/big enough/academic enough/business savvy enough/assertive enough/charismatic enough/disciplined enough/creative enough . . . or as good as your friend/colleague/predecessor/competitor . . .

3. Put you off

Combined with convincing you that you don't have what it takes, your monkey might also take a second line of attack to convince you that the quest you're considering is far too dangerous, impossible and completely not worth it.

It's too hard. It won't work. We tried it before remember? Don't bother, save yourself the headache and the heartache, love. Maybe another time, but not right now, hey? You don't have anything to prove. Give yourself a break . . .

4. Weigh you down

Your monkey might also try and remind you of all your other obligations: things you've already committed to, people who are relying on you, things you 'should' be doing.

Especially when you're working on something that matters to you, that perhaps no one else is going to chase you up on, your monkey may weigh you down with 'more serious responsibility' and try and put you off taking on that dream project that you'd really love to do.

5. Wear you down

'OK,' your monkey is thinking, 'if you're going to pursue this you'd better be armed with ALL the available information. Let's start with all the things that could go wrong. All the variables you have to get right. You call it disaster thinking, I call it being realistic and prepared.'

You might not be put off entirely but it sure takes a lot of energy to answer your monkey's questions. Remember decision fatigue? Every question you answer is another decision you have to make, another level of good judgement depleted. By the time you've finished going round in circles, you've forgotten what you were doing, notice it's nearly 5 o'clock and call it a day.

6. Fill your head with chatter

If the bullying and scare tactics don't work, your monkey might just throw a tantrum instead, and fill your head with a whole load of chatter. It might throw you a combination of put-downs and put-offs, some what-ifs and what-abouts, but all you can hear is a whole lot of noise.

Your monkey is just shouting, you don't have a clue what it's saying. It's loud and you can't think straight. Your brain simply freezes, gives up trying to do any amount of sensible thinking and goes on strike.

 **reflection**

What are your monkey's favourite tactics?

Dealing with your monkey

Do not fight the monkey.

Listen, the monkey is strong. You can't overpower it, and it is stubborn. It won't go away if you shout at it. In fact, the monkey loves shouting matches. It will happily shout back and keep shouting back. Fighting the monkey is exhausting, and doesn't work very well. Ignoring the monkey is also tricky. You can try and ignore it for a while, but when it keeps following you around tapping you on the shoulder, eventually that becomes torture.

What can you do instead? Here are some tactics to handle your mind monkeys:

Invite your monkey to play

Monkeys love games. So why not turn your work into a game? Tax return or expenses to do? Buddy up with an accountability partner and turn it into a competition. Hate confrontation but love puzzles? Turn it into a puzzle you're trying to solve. Earn the reward of doing something fun every time you do something difficult.

The Pomodoro Technique

When you have a whole day's work ahead of you, or a stack of work to get through, the thought of slogging through can be demotivating. The idea behind Francesco Cirillo's Pomodoro Technique is to work in dashes, to alternate 25 minutes of focus with a five-minute procrastination break.[3]

Take that big piece of work you keep putting off and start with a 25-minute stint, then give yourself full permission to move onto something else. Take the backlog of filing that's piling up, set your timer and see how much you can get through in 25 minutes (or 10 minutes if that feels more manageable – feel free to make up your own rules here!) Or take that presentation you know you could spend days tweaking, give yourself a limit and see how much you can get done in that time.

Eat that frog[4]

That thing you keep putting off – the one you'd really rather not do – that's hanging round like a bad smell. That's your frog. The frog follows you around every day, making you feel bad but not quite bad enough to actually do it. Every time you look at it your heart sinks. You pause and wonder how to tackle it, then move onto something a lot more doable. Every time you tick something else off the list, that sense of satisfaction is dampened by the fact that your frog is still there, taunting you and mocking you.

The idea is simple. If you eat a smelly, slimy frog for breakfast, everything you have afterwards will taste sweet. The game is to take one thing you've been putting off – one frog – and commit to tackling it first thing in the morning, before you do anything else. Before you get too tired, before you get distracted or waylaid, before checking your emails, or grab a coffee, or start chatting to colleagues, before something else crops up just get your head down for say 30 minutes and get it done. Before your monkey wakes up and starts shouting at you. Just do it.

The effect is brilliant. Not only is the frog gone and no longer haunting you (and probably didn't taste anywhere near as bad as you thought it would) but the boost to your motivation and self-esteem makes your monkey feel brilliant too.

 **brilliant** action

Identify one thing you've been putting off. Commit to eating that frog for breakfast tomorrow.

Dealing with FEAR

What do you find scary? Making sales calls? Giving presentations? Confronting a colleague?

Fear fuels resistance and steals enjoyment, contentment and satisfaction. Fear is the thing that has us saying:

- 'I know it's just . . . but I just can't seem to bring myself to do it.'
- 'I know I can, but I'm doing everything else to avoid it.'
- 'I know it's silly, but . . . anyway, I haven't got time now.'

A helpful acronym you can use to understand fear, is to see it as False Expectations Appearing Real. Our fear often turns out to be much bigger in our heads than it is in reality.

To replace your false expectations with reality, experiment with setting yourself some targets. Make five phone calls and log how you feel before and after the call. Revisit the positive feedback from the last presentation you gave. Or as Susan Jeffers suggested in the title of her book, *Feel the Fear and Do It Anyway*.

⤤)brilliant **reflection**

Where is fear holding you back? What would you discover if you faced it head on?

Just add fun

In the world of work, things can get a little too serious. And when things get serious, fear, overwhelm and procrastination come out to play.

Fun, on the other hand, is naturally motivating. It comes easy, it doesn't overwhelm and we don't need to psyche ourselves up for it. Fun engages our creativity and brings out our best ideas. It's easy to stay focused when you're having fun. You don't have to try. It just has you engaged. Distractions become less distracting. Procrastination is less appealing. Fun is sustainable. It's easy to keep going when you're having fun.

What would make it fun? Here are some ideas to get you started:

- Pair up and race a colleague to get your inbox to zero/ expenses submitted/tax return done.
- Set a stop watch or timer to see how fast you can work.
- Stand up to have that tricky phone call.
- Change the environment: go to a different room, escape outdoors, visit the art gallery, a café or the park . . .
- Start your breakfast meeting with hot bacon rolls – an added bonus to ensure everyone turns up on time.
- Move your meeting – literally. Go for a walking meeting: round the block for a quick update, into the forest for some deep discussions, or down by the beach (if you're lucky enough to work by the sea).

What would make it irresistible?

 **example**

My friend Jennie Harland-Khan runs her business around the concept of Irresistible Living.[5]

Instead of fighting resistance or making yourself do something you think you 'should', she asks: 'What would be an irresistible way of doing this?'

This question led Jennie to create her Irresistible Roadshow – overcoming her resistance to running webinars by hosting Google Hangouts from five different locations in two months: Morocco, Lanzarote, Chamonix, LA and Perth. How's that for irresistibility, huh? As a total travel fanatic, this solution was perfect for Jennie. She has shaped her own life and business around travelling, and she had reason to be in all those places anyway, so it wasn't a pipe dream. Suddenly something that she knew she 'should' do became something she couldn't wait to do.

Irresistibility overrides resistance. It might still be hard work or scary stuff, but when you turn up the irresistibility, that stuff stops stopping you. You power through the tough parts, put up with the mundane and find ways round the challenges because quite frankly, you can't wait to do it.

 **reflection**

What would make your something irresistible for you?

Devising your own game

Games get a bad press for distracting us from being produc-tive, but understanding how games work can also help us to come up with some creative and compelling ways of getting our work done. Helen Routledge, author of *Why Games are Good for Business*, suggests that there are three golden rules of game design that apply to productivity:[6]

1. Save the world, one step at a time

'Games are nested problems. They give you an overarching prob-lem to solve, say save the world, defeat the bad guy, build a city, but they don't tell you how to get there. They give you a long-term goal and it is up to the player themselves to work out how to get there. Also, a game doesn't just throw you in and say, "Hey dude, go and save the world", and then leave you to it. What actually happens is that you save the world through incremental tasks that individually may not seem so important but that actually come together to have a great impact. These are short-term goals.'

If you find yourself freaking out at a big goal, don't be put off if you can't see the whole path. Often the journey becomes clearer only when we start taking steps. Focus on the small steps that take you closer instead of trying to save the world in one fell swoop.

2. Don't forget the rewards

'Games always reward a player for doing something that moves them closer to the ultimate goal whether it's Experience Points (XP), new equipment, stars, coins or even just points, you always receive something for the effort you put in.'

My colleague gives himself a gold star for every Pomodoro he achieves. Graham Allcott suggests in his book *How to be a Knowledge Ninja* earning 'fun points' for every unit of study or work, then trading in those fun points for guilt-free pleasure: one point for an hour of watching Netflix, two points for coffee with a friend, nine points for a whole day off to spend as you please.[7]

3. Name your distractions as the bad guys

'Give them names and think about their powers. By identifying and labelling these distractions you'll start to notice when you're doing them more often.' Overcoming evil becomes a reward in itself. Which is precisely what we're doing here with mind monkeys, lizard brains and eating frogs.

What do you feed your monkey?

Your monkey craves quick hits. Scratching that itch to check your email, watching that cat video on Facebook, playing a quick round of Bejeweled. The problem is, these quick hits are like empty calories to your monkey. Monkey gets a quick high, and it feels good, but sooner rather than later it needs another hit, and then another, then another.

This is especially the case when your work is full of uncertainty. When you're working on that big project or that tricky situation where there's a lot of uncertainty and unknown – the monkey craves certainty. That's why you suddenly get an urge to go check email or tidy the stationery cupboard. The urge to do something simple and clearly defined is so tempting, we crave that bit of certainty, however unnecessary and pointless it may be. And it just gets worse. Just like a sugar addiction, the more instant hits your monkey gets, the more it craves. The more you feed the habit, the more it grows.

Starving your monkey is not an option. The key is to choose what you feed your monkey. Get it hooked on a diet of real satisfaction and reward, and your monkey will happily go along with you to work for the promise of that deeply satisfying feel-good banana it knows it's going to get at the end of the day. But to do that you have to hold up your end of the bargain. You have to let your monkey bask in the glory of 'job done' completion. If you rush straight back to 'what's next' and 'so much to do' your monkey will feel cheated and less likely to come along to play next time. Celebration, achievement and reward matter if you are to keep your monkey playing with you and primed for more.

As well as achievements, your monkey also feeds well on a healthy diet of feeling loved, contributing to a bigger picture and knowing that what it does matters.

Mood nudges

Here are some simple mood nudges that can nourish your monkey:

- Think about three things you are grateful for, or even better write them down.
- Remind yourself of 'something bigger' that you're part of – a movement, a team, a common purpose.
- Write down something you're proud of about yourself.
- Tell someone else why you're proud of them.

- Exercise – get those endorphins moving.
- Get outdoors, stock up on Vitamin D when the sun's out.
- Take a lunch break without your smartphone.
- Listen to music that lifts your mood.
- Learn something new.
- Do something just for the fun of it – no targets, no achievement, just have fun.
- Give someone something – a gift, a lift, a compliment, a smile, your full attention.
- Eat well.
- Remind yourself you are enough.

Ultimately an unhappy monkey will act up and cause havoc, while a happy monkey cheers you on and high fives you as you go.

 **reflection**

What do you need to stop or start feeding your monkey?

Don't wake the monkey

If you're careful you might not even have to deal with the monkey. The trick is to avoid sounding the alarm bells that would wake your monkey up. Bells that say THIS IS A BIG DEAL or THIS IS GOING TO BE HARD!

Baby Steps

A really effective way to tiptoe around your monkey without waking it, is to take Baby Steps. Take the big, scary projects that would have your mind monkey screaming and break them down into such small, insignificant steps that your monkey opens one eye, rolls over and goes back to sleep.

 **example**

If you were to tell me five years ago that I would be writing my second book on productivity, I would have laughed and told you you had the wrong Grace Marshall.

I am naturally disorganised and have never been good at being on time. So the fact that my first book topped the Amazon UK ranks for 'time management' still tickles me. Specialising in 'time management' or 'productivity' is not something I would have chosen myself. If you told me that's what I was setting out to do, I would have run screaming for the hills. But as a coach working with entrepreneurs who were juggling business and family, the biggest question that always came up was: 'Too much to do, not enough time. How do I fit it all in?' Being a mum of two small children myself, I knew exactly where they were coming from.

Answering that question, one client at a time, and working through it myself, sparked my passion (some would say obsession) with productivity. It wasn't until I was invited to be the 'Parent Productivity Expert' at John William's 'Screw Work Let's Play' programme that I tentatively embraced the 'expert' title, and even then I kept thinking, 'Any moment now, I'm going to get found out. I'm not the expert they think I am.'[8]

Turns out this is a pretty common phenomenon: Imposter Syndrome.

 **definition**

Imposter Syndrome
Describes the fear of being 'found out'. The worry that somehow you don't measure up, that you're not as good as people think you are. Researchers believe that up to 70 per cent of people have suffered from it at some point, including Kate Winslet, Don Cheadle and Maya Angelou. So if you get it too, you're in good company.[9]

That's where Baby Steps comes in.

Baby Steps mean you don't have to have it all worked out before you start. Instead of telling yourself you have to be the expert (which would be a big alarm bell to your mind monkeys), you can just focus on helping one person at a time, answering one question at a time, putting yourself out there one little risk at a time.

When you don't know if you have what it takes, Baby Steps can sneak past fear and confidence wobbles. Instead of being overwhelmed by the enormity of a project, Baby Steps can make things doable by breaking big hairy goals into small, specific steps you can focus on and absolutely achieve. No ambiguity, nothing else to work out, just plain, simple action. And because it's easy to get started when you're 'just' doing something really simple or small, Baby Steps are also incredibly effective for bypassing procrastination and creating momentum.

Baby Steps also means you don't have to wait until you have time. It's hard to 'find time' to do a big project, but it's easy to fit in a Baby Step here and there. That's how I managed to write my first book in 40 days, around my children, clients and other commitments. And that's how you can too – whether it's a book you want to write, a challenging target you want to hit, or a new career you want to break into. Extraordinary results come from taking seemingly ordinary steps every day in the right direction.

 'We are what we repeatedly do. Excellence, then, is not an act, but a habit.'

Aristotle

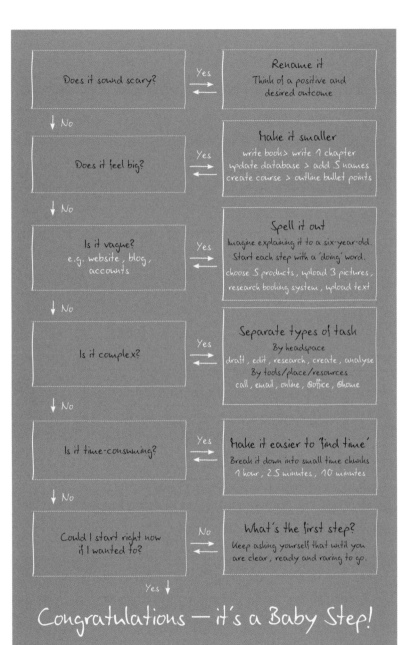

Does it sound scary? — **Yes** → **Rename it** Think of a positive and desired outcome

↓ No

Does it feel big? — **Yes** → **Make it smaller** write book > write 1 chapter / update database > add 5 names / create course > outline bullet points

↓ No

Is it vague? e.g. website, blog, accounts — **Yes** → **Spell it out** Imagine explaining it to a six-year-old. Start each step with a 'doing' word. choose 5 products, upload 3 pictures, research booking system, upload text

↓ No

Is it complex? — **Yes** → **Separate types of task** By headspace / draft, edit, research, create, analyse / By tools/place/resources / call, email, online, @office, @home

↓ No

Is it time-consuming? — **Yes** → **Make it easier to 'find time'** Break it down into small time chunks / 1 hour, 25 minutes, 10 minutes

↓ No

Could I start right now if I wanted to? — **No** → **What's the first step?** Keep asking yourself that until you are clear, ready and raring to go.

Yes ↓

Congratulations — it's a Baby Step!

 **brilliant** action

Take one big/scary project and use this checklist to break it into Baby Steps . . .

I'll just . . .

Another way of avoiding the alarm bells is to trick yourself into thinking that you're not really working. Mark Forster, author of *Do it Tomorrow*, suggests using the words 'I'll just . . .':[10]

- 'I'm not really going to [the task] right now, but I'll just do [its first step].'
- 'I'm not really going to write that report now, but I'll just get the file out.'

Try it for yourself:

- I'll just get the file out.
- It's just another conversation.
- I'll just scribble a few words.
- I'll just arrange a meeting.
- I'll just run it past one person.
- I'll just answer one question.
- I'll just see if I can help one person.
- I'll figure the rest out later. For now I'll just . . .

Seven alternatives to being right

When you're stepping into new territory, stretching outside your comfort zone or learning something new, the pressure to get things right can set off alarm bells that wake your mind monkeys.

 **example**

My son had a meltdown a couple of weeks ago over his homework. His class are transitioning to joined up handwriting, and his homework was to write a set of words in his best joined up handwriting. Like most things that are new, it feels awkward at first and doesn't come easy.

The more mistakes he made, the more frustrated he got. The more frustrated he got, the more mistakes he made. Eventually he had a complete meltdown with a whole heap of 'I'm rubbish' and 'I can't do it'.

We talked about why he was frustrated, and it came down to an overwhelming need to get it 'right'. It didn't look neat, therefore it wasn't right, therefore he had failed, therefore he was rubbish. That was his reasoning. That's was his monkey's line and he bought it hook, line and sinker.

I felt for him – because I know what it's like to be stumped by 'right'. I know what it's like to feel like I have to be right. To feel the pressure to get it right when everyone else around me seems to have it all worked out. Or to be the 'expert' who is expected to have the answers.

Sometimes right is the wrong thing to aim for.

Aiming for right can stop us from getting started, when it seems so far from our current reality. It can stop us from stepping into something new, where everything is unknown and uncertain and there is no 'right'. We can become too focused on having to have the right answers, that we forget to ask the right questions. We can be so obsessed with 'right' that we forget to have fun.

Sometimes we have to get things wrong in order to figure out what right even looks like. And sometimes the journey to right looks nothing like right.

Here are some alternatives to being right:

- **Be curious:** embrace the fact that you don't know. Be the one who's asking questions, rather than the one who has all the answers.

- **Be an experimenter:** the one who's testing, rather than the one who's being tested. Experimenting isn't about getting it right. It's just about doing, noticing and learning as you go along.

- **Be a curator:** some of the best 'experts' in the field are actually curators. People who bring together other people's experience and expertise, who capture the questions and the answers and weave together the stories and the knowledge in such a way that it brings new light to the subject.

- **Be a pioneer:** step out from what you know. Explore the unknown, the place where there is no 'right'. Seek new answers beyond the ones you already have. Go into unchartered territory and see what you discover.

- **Be the fool:** in olden days, the fool, or the jester, could speak the truth to the King when no one else dared. Precisely because they had no authority, agenda or expert status, they could say it exactly how they saw it. They could speak the truth and be heard. There is a freedom that comes with not knowing. With a fresh perspective that is unencumbered by prior knowledge, you can ask the silly questions, address the elephant in the room and bring the breath of fresh air that everyone's been waiting for.

- **Be practicing:** sometimes all it takes is practice. Fall down, get up. Try again. Rinse and repeat. Remember, everything that now comes naturally to us was at one point difficult and alien. Sometimes we have to let go of getting it right and just put in the practice. Instead of 'make it look perfect', my son's new goal became 'just fill the page'.

- **Be playful:** our creativity gets stifled when we take ourselves too seriously, when we put too much pressure on getting it right. We can get so caught up in that big scary goal that we forget to enjoy the process.

⚲ brilliant reflection

Where are you caught up with being right? Choose one alternative and try it on for size.

Conversations with your monkey

Listen up. What is your monkey actually saying? What does it need? What your monkey says it needs may not actually be what it needs.

- Is it panicking? Is it stood on a ledge convinced that the building is on fire? Do you need to talk it down?
- Is it insecure? Does it need reassurance and encouragement (rather than entertainment)?
- Is it being a drama queen? Does it need some calm, perspective and normality?
- Is it bored? Does it need some fun, purpose and passion?
- Does it feel backed into a corner? Monkeys tend to see things in black and white. Does it need some alternatives?
- Does it feel threatened? Does it need to know that it's safe to stand down?
- Is it feeling alone or out of its depth? Does it need to ask for support?

The reality check

Is your monkey getting carried away with disaster thinking and tall tales? Here are some tell-tale signs – spot the statements that start with these words:

● They say . . .
● Everyone thinks . . .
● It's always like this . . .
● You never . . .
● No one can . . .
● Nothing will change . . .
● It's all . . .
● That means . . .

If your monkey is in need of a reality check, here are some questions to ask yourself:

● 'What specifically went wrong?'
● 'Who says?'
● 'Always?'
● 'Never?'
● 'Give me a specific example. When has that been the case?'
● 'Give me an exception to that. When has that not been the case?'
● 'When might it work?'
● 'What if it did make a difference? Who would it make a difference to?'
● 'What hasn't gone wrong?'
● 'What am I making this to mean?'

 **action**

Document your mind monkey conversations. Write down what your mind monkey says, and use these questions to do a reality check.

The pep talk

Want to do a great job? Our first job is to put ourselves in a place where we can give our best. That includes the pep talk we give ourselves. If we let our monkey do the talking though, it could be a very different conversation!

 **example**

Ruth was procrastinating on her essay. Experience told her that if she left it too late she wouldn't be happy with what she submitted, but the feeling of self-doubt was so strong it was holding her back from getting started. Her monkey had a critical voice:

● 'I can't do it.'

● 'I won't be good enough.'

● 'I'm not academic enough.'

● 'I'm not disciplined enough.'

She knew there was plenty of evidence to show that she was clearly qualified and equipped to tackle this piece of work, but her monkey wouldn't shut up. There were a couple of essays in the past that she had left late and had 'fair feedback' which she wasn't entirely proud of. Her monkey had decided that it was best to avoid that 'awful feeling of being judged' for as long as possible. It was also quite a heavy and emotional subject matter, and her monkey was also trying to avoid the pain of diving in.   ▶

Her response to her monkey was 'that's dreadful!' She could see it wasn't helpful and she kicked herself for thinking it. However, monkeys don't tend to respond well to being kicked or berated. They don't like being told they're dreadful. They tend to act up even more.

So Ruth decided to do some reframing:

- She decided that if she was going to be judged anyway, she was going to choose to be judged on what she did do rather than what she didn't do.

- She shifted her perspective and focus from how she felt about doing the research ('I don't know if I'm ready, if I'm good enough, if I have what it takes . . .') to focusing on the subject matter ('This is heavy stuff, this is who it affects, how it happens, how it works, this is what I know about it . . .').

- She gave herself permission to feel emotional, rather than see it as a sign of weakness or an inability to cope.

- She changed her own critical voice – instead of berating her monkey with 'that's dreadful' and add to the emotion and drama, she simply identified it as 'unhelpful' and 'that's something I'd like to change'.

This helped her to focus on the research. By challenging the thoughts that were unhelpful and changing the conversation with her monkey, she shifted the block. Within one week of our conversation I got this message from her: 'I am now spending no time putting it off and more time enjoying and focusing on the research – Thank you!'

The rant and the reframe

Sometimes your monkey needs to have a rant, to express its fears and worries and feel listened to. This exercise lets your monkey do just that.

1 Grab two sheets of paper. In the centre of each sheet, write the name of the thing you're resisting, feeling demotivated about or stuck on.

2 On one sheet, give your mind monkey full permission to rant. Get all the unhelpful words and thoughts you have about

this out of your head and onto paper. Even if you know it's complete rubbish, if you're thinking it, write it down.

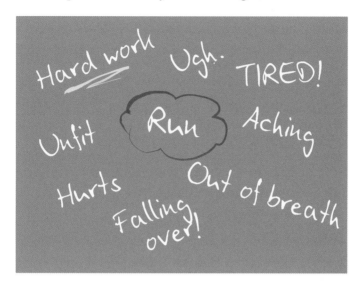

3 On the other sheet, collect and write down all the positive thoughts and helpful words that you associate with this thing.

I find these are most powerful when they come from a place of honesty. So if you want to write 'easy', but find that your instant reaction is to scoff at it, because you don't quite believe that yet, then try adding 'What if', for example, 'What if it's easier than I think?' or point it in the right direction e.g. 'getting easier'.

4   Then take a look at each sheet of paper. Notice the difference in how you feel when you look at each one.

What you notice grows. The more you notice something, the more there is of it to notice. And that has such an impact on how we experience things. Our thoughts and words shape our perspective. Our perspective shapes our experience. And all of this shapes what we choose to do next.

The beauty of this exercise is it's all about what's going on in your head. Which means you have full control. You can choose which one you focus on. Keep it visible, perhaps at the desk where you work, on the fridge or the mirror, or by your bed. Look at it and let the words soak in – before getting started, before you get up in the morning, or even last thing at night. Notice the difference.

Play the 'what if' game

'What if' can sometimes be used in an unhelpful way, to engage in disaster thinking. If you find your monkey saying, 'What if it goes wrong? What if I fail? What if everybody hates it?', try playing the 'what if' game.

First notice what your monkey is saying. Disaster thinking tends to go something along the lines of this:

1   What if . . . 'What if I mess up the presentation?'

2   Add meaning. 'I'd look a complete fool, I'd be letting everyone down, I'd lose the sale, my reputation would be

in tatters, there's certainly no way I'd be considered for promotion, and with the rumours of restructuring, I might even lose my job . . .'. This stage can last a while!

3   Add evidence. 'Remember THAT presentation? When you got the slides mixed up and you forgot your words? And that was a friendly audience. Did you hear what happened to the last guy who presented to this audience? They say . . .'

4   Turn 'what if' into 'what is'. 'I'm not a speaker. This isn't for me. It's not going to work. This is a terrible idea.'

 'Worrying is using your imagination to create something you don't want.'

Abraham Hicks

What if we used our imagination to create what we do want instead? The same skill can be used to build faith when we play the 'what if' game in a helpful way:

1   Come up with some positive, helpful 'what-if' statements. 'What if it goes better than I imagine? What if I am good enough? What if it's easier than I think? What if I really enjoy myself?'

2   Add meaning. 'It would be a great experience, I'd land the deal, inspire the team and set a great foundation to build on.'

3   Add evidence. 'Because I've done my research. I've built a good relationship. I am a good listener. Remember that time I really relaxed into my own shoes and they commented on how natural I came across?'

4   Turn what if into what is. 'I am good enough because . . . I will give this my best shot because . . . This is a great opportunity because . . .'

Mind your language

There are some words that monkeys seem to be particularly sensitive to. Simply changing some of those words can change the entire conversation. Here are some common ones:

But

- 'I'm confident in what I do, but running a business/ networking/public speaking is all new to me.'
- 'Website's lovely but the font's too small.'
- 'Written five chapters, but have twenty more to do.'
- 'I'm excited, but I'm scared.'
- '99 happy customers this week, but one complained.'

Notice how 'but' changes the tone of the story? 'We have good news . . . yay! But there's bad news . . . Oh pants.'

'But' has an effect of negating whatever came before. Good news gives way to bad news. Confident becomes not confident. Praise gets overshadowed by criticism. Progress leads to stuck. Done gets replaced by not done. Excited is overwhelmed by scared.

Replace 'but' with 'and'
- 'I'm confident in what I do and running a business/ networking/public speaking is all new to me.'
- 'Website's lovely and the font could be bigger.'
- 'Written five chapters and twenty more to do.'
- 'I'm excited and I'm scared.'
- '99 happy customers and one complaint this week.'

Notice the difference? Both parts of the sentence can exist alongside each other and have equal weight. In fact, the positive statement lends itself to the rest.

I'm confident *and* this is new. This is great *and* this is how it can be even better. This is what I've done *and* this is what I'm working on. Five down, twenty to go – progress all the way. I'm excited *and* scared – it's OK to be both. We got 99 right *and* one wrong – we did well *and* what can we improve?

Try it! Notice what happens when you say 'and' instead of 'but'.

'-ing' for work in progress

So often we focus on what's done and what's not done. What about the stuff in between? What about the work we're actually doing?

A friend once asked me, 'What are you working on?'

'How's business?' would have prompted a static answer: great/good/OK/not bad/could be better/awful/don't ask!

'What are you working on?' prompted a much more enthusiastic response. 'Well, I'm putting together a . . . and it's really exciting because . . . I'm still working out . . . and I'm looking forward to launching it in . . .'

Progress isn't static. So much of what we do is work in progress: building a business, raising a family, growing in confidence . . .

What are you working on? What are you creating? Where are you growing? What are you building on? What are you reaching? What are you celebrating? What seeds are you sowing? What harvest are you reaping? What reputation or relationships are you building? What are you transforming? What results are you seeing? And when you do take a snapshot and review what is done and complete, where is that leading you?

If you want the momentum and flow of being in progress, make sure your language has plenty of '-ing' in it.

'am' vs 'doing'

'I am' speaks to our identity. It feels permanent, part of who we are. 'I'm doing' describes an action, something we are taking part in, at this moment in time, which is temporary and detachable. So when clients say to me 'I'm a terrible procrastinator' I remind them procrastination is something you do, not who you are.

We can all *do* procrastination. How do you do yours? What do you say to yourself or out loud? What actions do you busy yourself with? What goes through your mind? What do you imagine? Where do you allow your attention to go? Once we know what we're doing, it becomes much easier to decide what to do differently.

'have to' vs 'get to'

'I have to' signals obligation and powerlessness. We have no choice, no control. We're trapped, there's nothing we can do about it. It often gets us playing the victim, 'There's nothing I can do about this' or the rebel, 'What do you mean I have to? No. I'm definitely not going to do it' (cue procrastination).

'I get to' signals opportunity and choice. We can choose in, rather than be forced to. It gets us looking for reasons why this might be a good thing. Take this example:

- 'I have to go to the gym so I can lose weight.'
- 'I get to go to the gym to lose weight.'
- 'I have to take the day off because my daughter's sick.'
- 'I get take the day off to look after my daughter.' (I get to be the one who holds her, to comfort her, I get to give her cuddles.)

 **example**

Rebekah found this little shift in words completely shifted her perspective. Her business was taking off and she had a lot of work coming in. 'I have all this work to do' was creating a feeling of resentment. She felt bogged down by her workload, deadlines, expectations and obligation. When she started saying, 'I get to . . .' she remembered that, 'Hey, I love my work! Look at all these lovely clients I get to work with, and these brilliant projects I get to work on.'

It can even change our perspective on the things we don't have any choice over:

- 'I have to pay this tax bill.'
- 'I get to pay a tax bill this year!' (I've actually made enough of a profit to have a tax bill!)
- 'I have to go to another meeting/make another presentation.'
- 'I get to influence the decisions and outcomes from this meeting/I get to represent my team and speak up for what we need/I get to get buy in from key stakeholders.'
- 'I have to deliver the bad news about the restructure.'
- 'I get to influence how this news is delivered. I get to be on the front lines, supporting and encouraging my colleagues during tough times.'

What are you currently telling yourself you have to do? What would your 'get to' statement be?

Can't

When you say 'I can't' what are you really saying?

That you don't know how? You don't have the resources to? That you're not sure you want to? That you're already committed to something else? Sometimes it's easier to say 'can't'.

'I can't make it' is easier to say (and more readily accepted) than 'actually I'd rather not' or 'I'd prefer to do something else' or 'I've already committed to something that I don't want to cancel'.

'I can't possibly do that' is easier to swallow than 'that scares me to death' or 'I'm not sure that would work' or even 'I don't know how to do that'.

When there's a risk involved, a cost, or a trade-off, 'can't' lets us off the hook. Rather than owning the decision, we default to 'can't' and it's out of our hands. The trouble is, after a while, we believe our 'can'ts' and they become the walls we build that hem us in. 'Can't' puts us in a position where we feel helpless. It signals impossibility and incapacity – so why bother trying?

---

brilliant example

I had a couple of conversations recently with friends who have made some pretty radical decisions about their businesses. Decisions they had previously said 'I can't' to.

- 'I can't take time off.'
- 'I can't raise my prices.'
- 'I can't do any more/less.'
- 'I can't do this in any other way (I've tried . . . it doesn't work . . . not for me/my business).'

But something changed when they hit a crisis. One had a health crisis that meant she had to take time off. Another was facing a personal crisis that meant that she had to make some tough choices. Instead of 'I can't' they both found themselves saying, 'This needs to happen. How do I make it happen?'

All of a sudden, 'I can't' was no longer an acceptable answer. Impossibility was out of the question. Everything was possible and something had to give.

Before, 'I can't' had them utterly convinced that there were no other options. Now, all the rules were thrown out, and they found themselves facing down hard choices, determined to find a way through, making tough decisions with courage, setting boundaries with ruthlessness and letting go of the need to please everybody and get everything right – because 'I can't' wasn't an option any more.

There's something about a crisis that gives us clarity. Clarity over what really matters. What's completely non-negotiable and what's up for grabs. But I wonder if we could create that clarity for ourselves more often, with less crisis, by being more truthful about our 'can'ts'.

Mindset trainer Caroline Ferguson suggests experimenting with this simple language tweak:

When you hear yourself say 'I can't . . . ', try seeing if one of these works instead:

- I choose not to . . .
- I haven't yet . . .

It sends a completely different message to your brain.[11]

Another alternative to 'I can't' is 'I don't'. For example:

- 'I don't work weekends.'
- 'I don't take calls after 5pm.'
- 'I don't cancel my gym appointments.'

Give it a try and notice the difference.

 reflection

Which words does your mind monkey tend to use?

 recap

When we find ourselves procrastinating, delaying, resisting or winding ourselves up, the chances are our mind monkeys have taken over. Understanding their monkey tactics can help us choose how we respond. Trying to fight or overpower our mind monkeys is a losing battle, but with some simple, creative tweaks to our perspective, language and behaviour, we can work with and around our monkeys to do our best work and have more fun doing it.

References

[1] Peters, S., 2012. *The Chimp Paradox*. Vermilion: London.

[2] Godin, S. 'Quieting the lizard brain'. Available at: http://sethgodin .typepad.com/seths_blog/2010/01/quieting-the-lizard-brain.html

[3] The Pomodoro Technique. Available at: http://pomodorotechnique .com

[4] Tracy, B., 2007. *Eat That Frog! 21 Great Ways to Stop Procrastinating and Get More Done in Less Time*. Berrett-Koehler Publishers: Oakland, CA.

[5] Irresistible Living. Available at: www.jenniehk.com

[6] Routledge, H., 'How game thinking can boost your productiv-ity!' [online] Available at: http://grace-marshall.com/how-game-thinking-can-boost-your-productivity/

[7] Allcott, G., 2015. *How to Be a Knowledge Ninja*. Icon Books: London.

[8] 'Screw Work Let's Play' was a 30-day challenge to start something you love in 30 days. Available at: http://www.screwworkletsplay.com

[9] Warrell, M., 2014. 'Afraid of being "found out"? How to overcome imposter syndrome'. Available at: www.forbes.com/sites/margie warrell/2014/04/03/impostor-syndrome/

[10] Forster, M., 2006. *Do it Tomorrow and Other Secrets of Time Management.* Hodder & Stoughton: London, p. 170.

[11] Caroline Ferguson, Mindset Trainer. Available at http://caroline ferguson.com/

CHAPTER 4

Prioritising your work and activities

How much of your daily work is actually productive action that produces real results? How much is taken over by busy work that just keeps you running faster on the hamster wheel?

This chapter focuses on techniques for evaluating your working-day activities, to distinguish between fake work and real work, practical tips to focus your best resources on what matters, instead of spreading yourself thin and diluting your impact, and how to stay productive even when you're procrastinating.

The new normal

How often do we answer the question 'How's it going?' with 'Busy!' Busyness has become the norm. But it has also become strangely aspirational. As much as we complain about being busy, we're also strangely resistant to being not busy.

When was the last time you heard anyone admitting to not being busy? That they had plenty of time, things were nice and slow, and they had plenty of spare capacity? Why are we afraid of the alternative? What would it mean to be not busy? Does that mean I'm lazy? Not doing enough? Will someone come and give me more work to do?

Busy can be seen as a measure of success. Busy means you're in demand, therefore you must be doing something right. If you're not busy, what have you done wrong? Admitting to not being too busy might land you with more work to do. You're on top of your work, are you? Great – go help Sally with her backlog! Or worse, maybe someone will start questioning whether you're surplus to requirements . . .

We might even feel resentment if someone isn't busy – that somehow they are not pulling their weight. If the rest of us are suffering, surely they should be carrying their piece of the burden too?

We validate our worth with busy. There's something about being busy that gets associated with being wanted, being needed, being in demand. Honestly, there's a part of me that enjoys being busy. I feel useful.

We use busy to judge whether we decide to do something or not – it seems more acceptable (or at least easier) to say, 'No sorry I'm busy,' than to say, 'Thanks but no thanks'.

We satisfy ourselves that we're doing the best we can because we're busy and couldn't possibly do any more. Or we feel like a constant failure because we're so busy trying to catch up.

Busy is seen as good work ethic. And those who aren't busy are viewed with suspicion.

Busy is our means of achieving, but also our excuse for not achieving. Not dealing with that problem that we've been avoiding. Not making that appointment to get that lump checked out. Not taking a break, or booking that holiday you keep promising yourself. Not going for that run, or that swim or that walk. Not having that difficult conversation with your partner, or your boss, or your kids. Not cutting your losses on the project that's not working out. Not letting go of that customer you've outgrown. Not being ruthless and saying no . . .

We know what we need to do, to manage our stress and stay healthy, but we don't do it because we're too busy. As the

American Psychological Association's 'Stress in America findings' 2010 report found: 'In general, Americans recognize that their stress levels remain high and exceed what they consider to be healthy. Adults seem to understand the importance of healthy behaviors like managing their stress levels, eating right, getting enough sleep and exercise, but they report experiencing challenges practicing these healthy behaviors. They report being too busy as a primary barrier preventing them from better managing their stress . . .'.[1]

Dr Susan Koven of Massachusetts General Hospital wrote in her 2013 *Boston Globe* column: 'In the past few years, I've observed an epidemic of sorts: patient after patient suffering from the same condition. The symptoms of this condition include fatigue, irritability, insomnia, anxiety, headaches, heartburn, bowel disturbances, back pain, and weight gain. There are no blood tests or X-rays diagnostic of this condition, and yet it's easy to recognize. The condition is excessive busyness.'[2]

How does this play out in your workplace?

- Do you honour the person who stays the latest or works the longest? Is there an unofficial competition for who has the largest to-do list? Mixed in with the sympathy, is there a certain sense of importance or admiration (or kudos) for the person who does the most?

- Do you secretly (or not so secretly) think more of the person who always says yes? Do you hold the mantra that 'if you want something done, give it to a busy person'?

- Does your workplace have an unspoken culture of honouring the person who leaves the office the latest?

Let's turn that around:

- Celebrate the person who does their best work in the fastest time, instead of the one who takes the longest.

- Give people the freedom to clock off early when they've had a super productive day.

- Measure work done by impact and results, rather than face-time.

 brilliant tip

Decide what 'job done' looks like at the beginning of the day. Give yourself a short, closed list to work from, then when you get to the bottom, consider your day's work done, and whatever time you have left over is yours to use as you choose. If you choose to work more, then consider that a bonus, over and above what was required for the day. If you choose to take the time off, do it with complete satisfaction that you've earned it.

From mindlessly busy to mindfully productive

'Nothing is less productive than to make more efficient what should not be done at all.'

Peter Drucker

Ever had a day where you know you've been super busy but if someone asked you what you've gotten done, you find yourself completely stumped for words?

Being busy isn't hard.

There's always plenty to do. Plenty of emails, calls to make, links to check out, events to research, industry news to keep on top of, requests from colleagues, ideas from your boss (not to mention your own brain), problems to fix, enquiries to answer, people to get up to speed, invoices to chase, someone to cover for, a last minute opportunity, a long-term project, deadlines that move, meetings to attend, notes to take, information to communicate, presentations to rewrite, data to analyse. Outside of work, there are appointments to make, buttons to fix, food to buy (and cook and clean up after), family to call, favours to do, friends to meet, bills to pay, talks to be had, presents to buy, parties to organise, people to look after, train tickets to collect.

Being busy isn't hard at all. What's hard is knowing what to not to do. When do you stop tweaking that manuscript and press send? When do you stop developing your product and actually put it out to market? When do you stop chasing those tiny leads and go for the big fish that scares you? When do you stop being so busy with the fake work and actually get on with the real work?

Impact thinking

True productivity is knowing what not to do, so you can genuinely commit to what you do do. So how do you decide? Here are some tools to help you to distinguish between what's worth doing, and what's perhaps worth less of your effort.

Pareto's Law

The story goes, that Pareto was an Italian economist, who was growing peas in his garden. When it came to harvest time, he noticed that 80 per cent of the peas came from 20 per cent of the pods. Like any good economist, he then applied that to everything else in life, and found that the same principle holds true: 80 per cent of a nation's wealth comes from 20 per cent of its population; 80 per cent of a company's profit comes from 20 per cent of its core customer base or core products or services.

Applying that to the work that you do, that means 80 per cent of your results comes from 20 per cent of your actions.

What's your 20 per cent? What's the work that you do that creates far more impact than everything else put together? And what would happen if you focused more of your time, energy and attention on your 20 per cent?

Where to apply this rule

Emails

Research suggests that email can take up to 28 per cent of our working day. How much of this is vital to your work? How much is noise? When it comes to email, the 80/20 rule can be more like the 800/20 rule. For every 20 pieces of useful email that is vital to their work, some people get almost 800 emails which may not be complete spam, but perhaps what we refer to as 'bacon': the somewhat useful, mildly interesting (perhaps even quite tasty) emails that fill your inbox. Common examples include:

- FYI
- CC
- group/global distribution lists
- office wide announcements: cakes in the kitchen, car parking notices, server maintenance
- out of office/holiday notices
- automatic notifications
- social media updates
- newsgroups
- newsletters
- industry updates
- sales emails.

Meetings

Would you be surprised if I told you that 33.91 per cent of all meetings are wasted, that 50 per cent of people find meetings to be unproductive and nine out of ten people daydream in meetings? Research suggests that executives spend an average of 23 hours per week in meetings, of which 7.8 hours are unnecessary and poorly run, which equates to two months per year wasted![3]

In his humorous six-minute TED talk, David Grady says, 'Every day, we allow our coworkers, who are otherwise very, very nice people, to steal from us . . . I believe that we are in the middle of a global epidemic of a terrible new illness known as MAS: Mindless Accept Syndrome. The primary symptom of Mindless Accept Syndrome is just accepting a meeting invitation the minute it pops up in your calendar. It's an involuntary reflex – ding, click, bing – it's in your calendar.'[4]

brilliant tip

Identify meetings you can respectfully decline or delegate the decision instead of being present to oversee them: 'Here are the parameters. I trust you – just let me know what you decide.' Ask: 'What's the purpose of the meeting? What do you need from me?'

David Grady suggests that when you show people you're interested in learning how you can help them achieve their goal, and do this respectfully and often enough, people will start to be a little bit more thoughtful about the way they put together meeting invitations – and you can make more thoughtful decisions about accepting it. If your contribution is only needed for part of the meeting, suggest that you only attend that part of the meeting. If you're calling a meeting, limit the numbers to only the people who absolutely need to be there. Challenge yourself to occasionally say 'Let's not meet!' and find another way to share the information or make the decision.

Ideas

Ideas are great, but it's only when we pursue them and put in the hard work that we actually create something of value. Saying yes to every idea can be exciting and fun, but a sure-fire way to run out of steam and never actually complete anything.

As Seth Godin challenges, 'Are you a serial idea-starting person? The goal is to be an idea-shipping person.'[5] It's only when you ship it, that it adds value. What good ideas can you say no to, so you can say yes wholeheartedly to the best ideas?

'Genius is one per cent inspiration, ninety-nine per cent perspiration.'

Thomas Edison

Delegating

How much of your time is spent doing something that someone else can do? What is that stopping you from doing?

 **definition**

Delegating
Letting someone else do what they can do, so that you can do what only you can do.

Action vs activity

Action takes you forward. Activity keeps you busy. Think about the work you've done in the last week. How much of it actually moved you closer towards your goals? How much of it just kept you busy?

 **action**

Separate your to-do list. How much of it is action and how much is activity? Are you clear which one is which?

Action	Activity

Some activity may be critical to keeping the wheels turning – your day-to-day job, delivering on existing commitments, keeping everything ticking over. But if your wider mission is to transform the business, move into a new market, get that promotion or qualification, go freelance or simply work less, then your actions are the ones that actually move you towards that goal.

You may not be able to eliminate all your activity (and indeed you might not want to) but if you don't seem to be making progress on any of your actions, perhaps you need to eliminate some of your activity to make space for the actions that matter to you.

What's in a name?

Project names can also help us identify what's worth doing. Generic project names like 'Website', 'Marketing' or 'Admin' do nothing for your focus, clarity and motivation. Here's why:

- **There's no defined outcome:** so how do you know when you've got there? It's hard to stay focused when you've got no finish line to focus on. And it's hard to get that 'job done' sense of satisfaction, or even a sense of progress, when you don't have a clue what 'done' looks like.

- **It becomes a dumping ground:** without a defined focus, generic projects like 'Website' can become an easy catch-all bucket for any tasks, thoughts or ideas that are remotely website related, but don't actually come together towards a common goal. Which means you either end up busily ticking things off with no real sense of direction, or get so overwhelmed that you shut the door on your dumping ground and turn your attention to something more manageable instead.

- **There's plenty of room for project creep:** you start off with plans for a simple website to showcase your expertise. Then you decide to add a blog, and a shopping cart . . . and some social media integration. Which means you need to revive your Twitter account . . . what about Pinterest? Maybe you'll add an interactive forum to the website, get people engaged . . . and really you should have some video . . . All potentially good ideas, but it doesn't matter how big the project grows, if you're not shipping anything, if that simple website remains un-launched, none of it makes any difference.

- **It's boring:** generic project names often feel boring, heavy, serious and too much like a chore. Like maths homework. Just thinking about it makes you groan and look for the nearest light relief to procrastinate with.

 **example**

That's the reason why I renamed my 'Admin' project 'Engine Room'. 'Admin' makes me want to run a mile, whereas 'Engine Room' reminds me that this is the stuff that keeps my business running and ticking over. It may not be pretty, and I might have to get my hands dirty, but it's sure as heck vital if I want to carry on playing above deck, and that gives me the motivation to roll my sleeves up and get stuck in, elbow deep in accounts and paperwork.

brilliant action

What about you? Do you have any generic projects on the go at the moment? Have a go at renaming them. Think positive, desired outcome. Be clear, be decisive. And be playful – choose a name that excites you – and see what that does for your focus and momentum.

Here are some great project names I've come across:

- Reclaim Living Room
- Home Sweet Home
- Enjoy Christmas
- Revive Team Spirit
- Make Sally Laugh
- Wonderful Work Place
- Make the Boat Go Faster.[6]

The perfectionist's curse

 'The last moments spent on anything are rarely the most valuable.'

Graham Allcott[7]

The curse of the perfectionist is that we know exactly what perfect looks like but never attain it, while 'good enough' is attainable, but kind of hard to define. Somewhere between 'good enough' and 'nearly but never quite perfect' is the territory where real work becomes fake work. Where thinking becomes overthinking. Analysing becomes overanalysing. Writing becomes excessive. Checking becomes obsessive.

What makes it difficult to tell is that every extra ounce of effort we put in probably does create a tiny drop of real value, but the closer we get to perfect, the more effort it takes and the less value it creates. It's up to us to work out the pay-off. Do I spend all day getting this perfect? Or do I spend half the time doing a good enough job, then move onto the next thing?

Athletes at the top of their game probably spend an inordinate amount of time perfecting their game, but in order to do this, there will be other things they will need to do to a much lower standard. We can achieve extraordinary things as long as we accept other things to be ordinary. We can certainly excel in a few choice things, but not everything can be – or needs to be – done to a gold-plated standard. Some things are fine being silver-plated, bronze-plated or just plain done.

Your choice.

Less is more

Great editors and designers know that what they remove adds value to what remains. Saying less can sometimes have a bigger impact. An unhurried cup of tea can be far more pleasurable than an elaborate banquet. Doing one thing well can bring far more satisfaction than doing a hundred things badly. A five-sentence email gets read and replied to far quicker than an essay. A three-minute video can be much more memorable than a three hour lecture. In our crowded lives, space is the thing we hunger for more than stuff.

Fake work vs real work

Some fake work is easy to spot: watering the plants, staring into space, fiddling with the spreadsheet, designing yet another tri-fold brochure, spending hours reading non-important emails.

Some feels like genuine hard work, and it is, but maybe that's all it is. Hard work that doesn't take you anywhere. Hard work that just keeps your wheels spinning, going nowhere fast. Hard work that keeps you busy rather than move you forward.

Fake work could be:

- working on the fifth iteration of the new brochure rather than picking up the phone to that customer
- doing more research when you know you should be delivering
- adjusting the font or re-reading 'just one more time' instead of pressing publish
- playing email ping pong instead of picking up the phone
- building another spreadsheet model instead of getting investors in
- having another meeting instead of making the decision
- weighing in with your opinion on another colleague's problem, instead of working on what you really need to figure out
- rewriting your to-do list
- making a list of people to call
- analysing who to call (until you run out of time to call them).

Ditching the fake work – removing the temptation

Graham Allcott, author of *How to be a Productivity Ninja*, has a theory that productivity is a battle, between the two very different versions of you: the lazy, scatterbrained you vs the

clever, motivated you. The lazy, scatterbrained you jabs away
at you, distracting you, tempting you, wearing you down. But
the clever motivated you can deliver some pretty strong sucker
punches that can disarm the lazy scatterbrained you. These are
known as power moves:

- Turning email notifications off on your phone and desktop
  is a power move that saves you all those pings and pop
  ups calling to you.

- Putting your phone on charge downstairs, and getting an
  old-fashioned alarm clock is a power move that removes
  the temptation to take your work to bed.

- Setting a deadline and making yourself publicly
  accountable is a great way of putting a limit on your
  procrastination and perfectionism. A deadline in someone
  else's world makes a target much more real and powerful.

 **action**

List the fake work you are most likely to get tempted into. Identify one
power move for each one.

Fake work	Power move

Preparation vs procrastination

When does preparation become procrastination? When it replaces the work instead of enabling it.

 **example**

This is how author Janice Horton described her writer's procrastination:

I tend to get immediately side-tracked on my way to my desk and I find that I'm giving other jobs (housework or cooking mostly) priority over what I should be doing (writing my books). It's as if I have to get the other things out of the way, in order to 'clear my mind and my workspace' and concentrate fully on my writing. Often, by the time this happens, I'm physically and mentally tired![8]

Clearing space both mentally and physically to work can be a really useful thing. But when it takes over and replaces your work, that's not so helpful! The truth is, there's always stuff to do. There's always another job to do, another pile to tidy, another thing to remember, another email to answer, if you wait until 'everything' is done before you start writing, you'll never start.

The same goes for that pile of emails, meeting notes or colleague requests you feel compelled to clear out of the way, before you start on your own work. Or the amount of research you want to do before you feel confident presenting your idea to your boss.

The trick is to limit your preparation. Give yourself say 15–30 minutes to get your space in order. This will get you deciding what absolutely needs to be in place during that time, (e.g. pen, paper, laptop, cup of tea, urgent disasters averted) and what can wait until later (e.g. the report for next week's

meeting, phoning the bank, replying to emails). Use a timer if
you need to.

 **definition**

Preparation enables work. Procrastination replaces it.

Real work doesn't always feel like work

Just as fake work can sometimes feel a lot like work, real work
sometimes doesn't feel like work at all. In fact, it may even feel
like you're wasting time.

Thinking time

When things are busy, it can feel like you don't have time to
stop and think. In fact, thinking can feel like you're wasting
time. You want to get on with the work, and thinking doesn't
feel like work. But thinking is where we define the work,
decide the what, when, why and how of work. Thinking can
make all the difference between a productive day and busy day,
between meaningful work and meaningless chore, between us
doing the work and the work doing us. Thinking is the most
important work you do.

Recharge time

Whether it's time to rest, have fun, indulge, or let your mind
freewheel, if it recharges you, and restores your capacity to do
your best work, it is one of the most productive things you can
make time for. As human beings, we are not designed to function non-stop without a break. Our brains get bored, tired and
lose focus. We stop being able to do our best work, to think
strategically, logically, creatively, and instead just go through
the motions.

The problem is, taking a break feels unproductive. And the part of us that subscribes to the busy culture tells us we're slacking. We feel guilty. In a study commissioned by Staples, a study of office workers and managers revealed that even though an overwhelming majority of workers (86 per cent) acknowledge that taking a break would make them more productive and 90 per cent of employers say they encourage breaks, more than a quarter of workers don't take a break other than lunch, and one in five employee respondents cite guilt as the reason they don't step away from their workspaces.

Asking silly questions

If you're worried about making a fool of yourself or wasting someone else's time, start with, 'Can I ask a silly question?' Often the answer is yes. More often than not, it's not a silly question at all. If nothing else, it will give you clarity instead of confusion. And once in a while, the blindingly obvious turns out to be brilliantly helpful.

Letting someone else do it slower . . . or even badly

The early days of letting someone else learn the ropes are painful. It's great when others can do what they can do, so you can do what only you can do, but getting there takes time. It can be tempting to take over, especially when time is tight and things are busy. But the more you can let them learn and practise, the more capable they will become, and the more that frees you up to do what only you can do.

Blank space in the diary

When time is limited, it's tempting to cram something into every nook and cranny, the way a budget airline packs people in like sardines. It feels inefficient to leave gaps. But gaps give us room to manoeuvre, and margin to adapt to the unexpected. Building margin into our day is precisely the thing that helps us to stay productive in a fast-changing, unpredictable world. And if you've had the budget airline experience, you'll know that breathing space itself adds massively to the quality of our day.

More than what you do

When we're busy fighting fires and meeting deadlines, investing in ourselves – our personal and professional development – can often be the first thing to fall off the list.

Your job is more than what you do. You are more than what you do. If you are a teacher, how you show up in the class-room will affect how you inspire those kids and what kind of role model you become. As a speaker, the energy you bring into the room, and how you deliver your talk will affect what people take away. The value you bring, your life's work, your immediate impact and your lasting legacy depend as much on how you show up – who you bring into the room – as what you do.

brilliant tip

Invest in your productivity by investing in you – what would enable you to show up at your best, so you can do your best work?

What are you building?

Everything you do accomplishes two things: the thing you do, and the thing you build. For example, saying yes to one job builds your reputation in that area. Every job you do builds your reputation. Is that the direction you want to build your career or business?

Answering the question for the fifth time answers the question, but it also builds a precedent. It makes you more likely to be the oracle in your organisation – the person people are likely to turn to before they ask Google. Responding to an email on a Sunday afternoon may be a one-off thing, but it also sends a signal that you may be accessible on a Sunday afternoon, and that can start to build an expectation. Every act builds a habit. And when individual habits come together they become culture.

The fine art of faffing

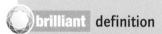 **definition**

Faffing
The art of keeping busy (usually with unimportant things) so you can avoid doing the thing you really should be doing.

Let's face it we can all do it. That quick check of your emails, the snatched water-cooler conversation, hanging around on social media a bit too long, popping over to a colleague's desk for a quick catch-up. Make a list, make a cup of tea, change the list. Tweak the font. Make it look pretty. Change your mind. Open up that project. Rearrange the papers. Put it down again. Make another cup of tea. Check your phone. Check your email. Check the brief again. See if anything's changed . . .

They say that fight or flight is our body's natural response to stress. Perhaps freeze and faff should also be in there somewhere. Sometimes when the workload is high, our response is to faff. To feel like we're doing something, because the thought of doing nothing is unbearable, but the thought of doing *the* thing is too painful.

There are times when we do need to just stop it. Stop. Faffing. Around. Close down your inbox. Turn off your phone. Lock yourself in a room. Tell your colleagues not to talk to you until that thing is done.

But let's not fool ourselves. Not 100 per cent of our time can be spent in high-production, high-performance mode. And indeed, it shouldn't be. True productivity is about harnessing the highs and the lows, not coasting on mediocrity.

So if we're going to faff anyway, let's master the fine art of faffing.

Productive procrastination

There are times when our brains just need a break. When staring at the screen is blatantly not working. If you're going to procrastinate, you might as well procrastinate well.

Two projects on the go

Does your inner rebel procrastinate more when you force yourself to focus? Try having two projects on the go:

---

brilliant example

Marianne often works with two projects on the go. When one feels too heavy or boring, she flips over to the other one. Her mind monkey is happy because it thinks she's procrastinating. The other project is a playground to avoid doing the work. When that project starts to feel too much like hard work, she switches back to the first one. By bouncing round between the two, she never feels 'forced to work' and always makes progress, whether she feels like she's working or not.

Pick and mix

Switching between large tasks and quick wins, or between different types of tasks, can be incredibly effective. If you've

spent ages typing away and you're craving some human contact, all of a sudden that follow-up call you've been putting off
won't seem so bad after all. If you need a break from mental
heavy lifting, doing some brain-dead filing is perfect. If staring
at a spreadsheet is making your eyes go funny, go for a walk
and take one of your 'thinking' tasks with you. That way you
restore your sanity and focus, while getting something else
done too.

brilliant example

I love it when my husband works from home. Miraculously all the little
jobs that have been hanging around for weeks suddenly get done: the
door handle that needs fixing, the bulb that needs replacing, the car part
that needs ordering, the lawn that needs mowing. Because when he's
procrastinating, he looks for something useful to do. Something not too
taxing, something that gives him a quick hit, preferably something physical
if his brain's tired.

The trick is to have this stuff ready to pick up when you need
to. Keep your 'quick win' files to hand or your tool box by your
desk. Use categories like @thinking or @zombie in your to-do
list to batch up these kinds of tasks so you can easily access
them when you need to switch focus – instead of accidentally
ending up on YouTube or at your colleague's desk discussing
the election results.

Your 'pick me up' playlist

What do you do when you're feeling fed up? When you look at
your to-do list and feel a bit 'meh'? Do you find yourself stuck
in limbo land, trudging away halfheartedly, not really working
but not not working either? Do you drag yourself to your seat,
only to stare at the screen for an hour? Or do you do something
that picks you up and gets you back on track?

 action

Create a 'pick me up' playlist - a list of energisers that boost your mood, kickstart your motivation, and gets you inspired and moving again. They could be big things or little things. In fact, tiny things work exceptionally well. They could include, but are definitely not limited to:

● music

● fresh food - instead of reaching for the nearest comfort junk

● getting outside - for a walk, a run, or just a breath of fresh air

● activities that energise you

● conversations, blogs or TED talks that inspire you.

Wasted time

 'The time you enjoy wasting is not wasted time.'

Bertrand Russell

Sometimes the thing that keeps us trudging along in busy mode is the fact that we feel guilty if we're wasting time. However, if it is time you truly enjoy spending – daydreaming, napping, chatting, doing nothing – and it restores your capacity to do good, worthwhile, meaningful work, then perhaps it's not wasteful at all. At the end of the day, your time will only feel productive if what you spend it on is personally meaningful. What is productivity after all, if it's not about making space for what matters?

If you tick lots of things off the list that don't matter to you, that won't feel satisfying. If you meet with lots of people but can't remember a single conversation, none of it will be meaningful. If you make lots of money but never get to spend it, is that truly valuable? If you have time (and you do), but never enjoy it, frankly what's the point?

When you get to the end of the day, instead of asking yourself, 'What have I done?' try asking yourself:

- 'What am I proud of?'
- 'What did I especially enjoy?'
- 'What did I relish?'
- 'What am I grateful for?'
- 'What made a difference?'
- 'What surprised me?'
- 'What were the moments that mattered?'

⚲ brilliant reflection

No one can tell you what your fake work and your real work is. Only you can decide. Real work feeds you: it gives you a sense of satisfaction, that you're contributing to something that matters to you. Fake work steals your energy and your time, and gives you very little in return.

It's up to you to decide which is which in your world. And how much of your life you devote to each.

⚲ brilliant recap

Being busy isn't hard, and if we're not careful, we can end up working so hard that we are 'too busy' to do our best work. When we stop honouring busy, we can start focusing on impact, results, progress and what matters. When we stop to think, we can clearly identify between activity that keeps us busy, and action that actually moves us forward. When we resist the temptation to keep ourselves busy with fake work, we make space for our real work, and our best work, and surprise ourselves with how much we achieve.

References

1 American Psychological Association, 2010. 'Stress in America findings'. Available at: www.apa.org/news/press/releases/stress/2010/national-report.pdf

2 Koven, S., 2013. 'Busy is the new sick'. Available at: www.boston.com/lifestyle/health/blog/inpractice/2013/07/busy_is_the_new_sick.html

3 Pidgeon, E., 2014. 'The economic impact of bad meetings', TED. Available at: http://ideas.ted.com/the-economic-impact-of-bad-meetings/

4 Grady, D., 2013. 'How to save the world (or at least yourself) from bad meetings', TED. Available at: www.ted.com/talks/david_grady_how_to_save_the_world_or_at_least_yourself_from_bad_meetings

5 Godin, S. 'Random rules for ideas worth spreading'. Available at: http://sethgodin.typepad.com/seths_blog/2010/01/random-rules-for-ideas-worth-spreading.html

6 'Will it make the boat go faster? Olympic-winning strategies for business success'. Available at: www.willitmaketheboatgofaster.com

7 Allcott, G., 2014. *How to be a Productivity Ninja: Worry Less, Achieve More and Love What You Do*. Icon Books: London.

8 'How to beat writer's procrastination'. Available at: http://grace-marshall.com/how-to-beat-writers-procrastination/

CHAPTER 5

Being productive and working with others

n an ideal world, we'd get ourselves perfectly organised, know exactly what we need to do, be 100 per cent focused, get it done, and go home. In the real world, however, we have to work with and around other people's priorities, schedules, expectations, delays and last-minute emergencies.

In reality, none of us works in a bubble. We work with other people. We rely on other people in order to get our work done well. Colleagues, co-workers, customers, suppliers, partners, bosses, staff, stakeholders – and everyone has their own agendas, priorities, schedules, expectations and ways of working. We also work in imperfect situations. Project deadlines that were way too tight to begin with. Emergencies we failed to scope. Delays we didn't plan for. Curveballs and changes beyond our control.

This chapter delivers techniques for managing your attention, availability and expectations in a team environment, conversations to encourage good communication, productive teamworking and effective firefighting as well as tactics to manage upwards, if you find that the chaos comes from the top.

Managing your attention

Imagine you're deep in thought, writing a report, figuring out next quarter's strategy or juggling formulas on a spreadsheet. Your colleague appears at your desk.

'Is now a good time? Have you got a minute?'

Whether you say yes or no, the chances are they've already interrupted your flow of thought, and you know it will take much longer than a minute to recover your attention, get back into your flow of thought and pick up where you left off.

Open offices can be great for collaboration, social interaction, building relationships and creating an energising buzz to work in, but they can also be the number one killer of focused attention. In the days when we all worked in separate offices, we could close the door as a 'do not disturb' signal. Nowadays, with open offices, we need to be a bit more creative.

Do not disturb

 **example**

Think Productive's COO Elena Boga has a china cat that goes on her desk when she needs to have some uninterrupted time to herself. When the cat's on the desk, it's her way of saying, 'I need to focus right now. Unless it's an emergency, could you come back later please?' When the cat's away, she's happy to be interrupted. Other people use headphones, traffic light signals, flag systems, signs, or even hide behind a plant.

How to set up your 'do not disturb' signal

1 **Choose your signal.** Will you use headphones, traffic light signals, a sign, flag system or something else?

2 **Communicate.** The key to making this work is communication. Explain that there are times when you need to have your brain to yourself, when you're not likely to be able to give anyone else your best attention or your best answer. Show them what you're going to use as

your 'do not disturb' signal, instead of expecting them to guess, and reassure them that there will be times when you will be fully available. Your conversation might start something like this: 'If the building's burning down, do interrupt me! But if it's not an emergency, and I've got my headphones on, could you just hold that thought and come back to me later? When the headphones are off, I'm all yours.'

3 **Remind and refine.** It can take time and practice for people to get used to a new way of working. Don't let one person's 'I forgot' deter you. Some people may need a little bit more training than others. Others may need some forewarning. Keep reinforcing, revisiting and refining your 'do not disturb' signal and how you communicate it to others.

You may find when you have this conversation, that it prompts or gives others permission to do the same. We all have times when we need to have our brains to ourselves – you might just start a trend in the office!

brilliant tip

If you use an internal messaging system like Lync, you can set your status to 'do not disturb', which means that you can still send Instant Messages, but others cannot initiate a conversation with you. If there are a select few you want to give the power to override that 'do not disturb' to, change your privacy relationship with that contact to 'Workgroup'.[1]

Stealth and camouflage

There may be times when you do need to be a bit more 'hidden' than having a 'do not disturb' signal at your desk. This is where tactical hiding can be quite handy.

Physically being out of the office or away from your desk can give yourself that extra 'space' to focus. For some people it's the only way to ensure they get to focus their attention on their own agenda, rather than constantly responding to others.

Some people use a meeting room, work from home, go to another part of the office or a different office altogether. Others go to a café, an art gallery or the local library.

If you're going to disappear for a while though, you might want to communicate this so everyone knows what to expect. Otherwise, if you develop a reputation for being too hard to find, it could backfire on you and you could end up playing an elaborate game of corporate hide and seek instead.

 **example**

Think Productive CEO Graham Allcott once sent an email to say that he was going to be 'off the grid' for a week to write his book:

Hi all,

Just a quick note to say next week I'm going dark, to write a big chunk of the 'Introducing Productivity' book.

So I'll be off all social media, email and phone for the whole week. I'm around all of this week if you need stuff though.

And then back on Monday 3rd March.

Graham

Instead of just disappearing off the face of the earth, he gave advance notice and made himself available the week beforehand, so if there was anything people did need to talk to him about, they could raise it before he disappeared.

You can also practise stealth and camouflage by electronically unplugging. Turn off your email, social media – or even switch off your internet connection altogether. Put your phone on divert, and see how much you can get done in an hour of uninterrupted time, compared to a whole day of being interrupted.

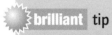 **tip**

Use Twitter, Lync or Skype to create accountability as well as stealth and camouflage by declaring what you're working on, and when you're committed to working on it: e.g. 'Working on Project X today 10.00–12.00. Back in communication this afternoon'.

Agendas

When there's someone you work closely with, it's easy to get into the habit of firing off questions when they come to mind and end up constantly interrupting each other.

brilliant action

Think about the five people you work closest with. Invite them to try this experiment.

Instead of interrupting each other as and when the thought occurs, keep a running agenda of all the things you want to discuss with them - and ask them to do the same for you. Agree a set time when you will get together to run through agendas (e.g. once a week) or a set number of items (e.g. 'Let's talk when we have five things on the agenda').

Managing your availability

How available are you? Do you have email on 24/7? Does your phone buzz when someone tweets you? Do you wake up to that familiar red light flashing on your Blackberry? What about times when you're in a meeting? With a client? On the phone? When you're travelling, driving, at a conference or attending training? When you're off work? On holiday, with your kids, on a date, in the bath or asleep?

Whether you like it or not, there will be times when you're not available to answer emails – and probably arguably plenty more times when you could do with being less available. Yes there's often an expectation that email requires a quick, or even instant response. Yes, some industries and organisational cultures actively perpetuate this expectation. But how much of that expectation do you set for yourself?

Here are some examples of how you can actively manage expectations.

Email signatures

You can use your email signature to communicate your working hours or likely response time.

 **example**

Paula Levett, our Client Happiness and Logistics Manager, has this on her email signature:

Please note we run a 'Four-Day Working Week' here at Think Productive, so I am out of the office most Fridays. If your issue is urgent, please call the office line below.

And Matthew Brown, our London Ninja has this:

I check emails once a day. If your matter is urgent, please call me. I am unavailable by phone and email on Fridays.

This can also work well with job share and part-time workers, as well as people whose job involves travel, different office locations or days in meetings. Being upfront about your availability means people know when they can get hold of you. It also means that they can pre-plan. If there's something you need from Paula or Matthew before the end of the week, ask them before Thursday's out.

Email autoresponders

Email signatures are great for setting ongoing expectations or when you are making the first move, but if you need to set an expectation about your response time to incoming queries, an autoresponder might be more useful.

brilliant example

If your role requires you to dive deep with focused attention as well as being responsive to customers you could take your inspiration from this accountant's email autoresponse:

Thank you for your email. I am likely to be in a meeting or immersed in a client's work. So that I can give them my undivided attention and focus, this inbox is checked once a day. If you need me more urgently than this, please text or leave a voicemail on my mobile xxxxx and I shall respond to you as soon as I am free.

Or for a more humorous approach, this is one recruitment consultant's email autoresponse:

Thank you for your email.

Those that know me well will realise that the remnants of childhood hyperactivity mean that I can be distracted by the slightest thi . . . ooohhhh, look, a chicken!

To be more effective, and ultimately serve you better, I am only accessing emails at 12.00 pm and 4.00 pm daily. If your issue is urgent and requires my immediate attention then please call me.

Thank you for your cooperation.

Often when we send an email all we want to know is that it's in hand and to know when we'll get a reply – instead of wondering if/when we need to chase. Knowing with confidence that someone will get back to me within 24 hours allows me to park it on my waiting list (see page 16) and forget about it for the next 24 hours, rather than play a lottery of wondering if it will be a super-fast two-minute response or whether it will take weeks of chasing. And, of course, offering an alternative for emergencies covers the more urgent requests – which are usually far less common than we think.

Voicemail

Worried about appearing rude, impersonal or unhelpful if you let calls go to voicemail? The problem is it can be equally rude (and arguably more so) if you take a call when you're supposed to be giving someone else your undivided attention, so why not be clear about that?

brilliant example

If you call my mobile and get my voicemail, you'll hear something along the lines of:

Thanks for calling, I'm probably with a client right now, helping them to replace stress and overwhelm with playful, productive momentum. If you'd like me to do the same for you, leave me a message and I look forward to speaking with you soon.

I never feel guilty about letting calls go to voicemail, because it usually makes people smile, doubles up as a marketing message and lets my clients know that when they are with me, they get my undivided attention.

Open office hours

Some doctors have an 'open surgery' during certain hours of the week. If you need to see a doctor and don't have an appointment, just turn up, take a number and wait in line. Equally, you could offer open office hours for your clients or colleagues, when people know they can come to you for ad hoc support.

brilliant tip

For scheduled appointments, an online tool like Timetrade can sync with your own calendar and allow people to choose from available slots rather than play email ping pong to get a date in the diary.

If you're out of the office a lot and your team find it hard to track you down, you might find it helpful all round to let people know when you're in and when you're available to avoid being pounced on when you reappear: 'I'm travelling on Monday, in meetings Tuesday to Thursday, and back in the office on Friday.'

Afternoon tea

brilliant example

June Dennis, Head of University of Wolverhampton Business School, schedules 'afternoon tea' sessions for her students. She will let them know a time and place each week where she is available to answer any questions and discuss their work. She'll even buy them a cup of tea.

This means her students know exactly when and where to find her, without having to hunt down her office and hope for a suitable time, and she gets ▶

to be less 'in demand' during the rest of the week. It also means she can also give them her full attention during that time – and has often found these to be incredibly useful conversations, where she finds out far more about her students – who's pulling all-nighters and surviving on caffeine, who's dealing with bereavement, who's struggling with home sickness – and can signpost them, advise or encourage them much more than in snatches of conversation when she's busy.

Keeping everyone updated

Why do people have update meetings? Seriously, what's the point? The worst ones are where everyone just has their say – where everyone's agenda is just to fill their slot with some kind of an update – usually along the lines of 'this is what I've been busy doing'. But what does, 'Can I have an update?' even mean?

Dr Penny Pullan of Making Projects Work says, 'The most effective project updates are about two-way communication, not just pushing out information. They ensure that people know what they need to know and can feedback to you. There are no nasty surprises! First of all, you need to understand who you are updating. What does success for your project mean to them? What are their communication needs?'[2]

The accountant's definition of success may well be different from the marketing director, and as such, they will want to know different things. People have different preferences depending on their personal style and level of involvement. Where one person might want a detailed briefing each week, someone else may only want the headlines once a month. Knowing those expectations upfront can make your life easier (less mind-reading!) and your updates more meaningful.

A communication plan essentially boils down to these factors:

- Who needs what?
- By when?
- What format?
- How often?
- Are you going to keep records?

Once you know this, you can decide what an update could look like, for example:

The super quick update

- Here's what we achieved last day, week etc. Here's what we're doing now. Please help us with . . .
- What questions do you have?

The more comprehensive update

- Progress: what's done, what's on track, what's changed, what's next.
- Impact: What this means for you.
- Requests: What I need from you/Please help us with.
- Next actions: Who's doing what next.
- Questions: What questions do you have?
- Next check in: already in the diary/arrange date in diary now.

Get visual

Your update might not even be full of words. Sometimes visual cues can be much more effective than lengthy documents or meetings. For example, the London 2012 Olympic Games update consisted of a single A3 colour sheet that showed the status of multiple projects, using traffic light colours to track the performance of each project: Red (significant issues), Amber (potential problems that need attention) and Green (going as planned).

---

brilliant tip

How else could you give your update and invite questions? A three-minute video? A walking meeting? An internal client/project management system?

The daily huddle

Instead of lengthy team meetings, try a daily huddle – a ten-minute quick start to the day where you ask each other:

● What's your good news?

● What are you working on?

● Where are we up to with the numbers and targets in the business?

● What are we stuck on?

● Are we OK for tomorrow's huddle, is anyone not here tomorrow?

It's great for bringing everyone together, reminding them what's most important and encouraging good communication, and often flags up any hot potatoes, things that need further discussion, opportunities for collaboration and who might need some extra help that day.

Productive conversations

Just as our individual productivity depends on the quality of our thinking and habits, our team productivity also depends on the quality of the conversations we have as a team. Here are some useful conversations which can make a big difference to your team productivity:

What do we need to let go of?

'Listen up, guys, we've got a new client/project/opportunity . . .'. New opportunities come up, new clients, new projects, new ideas. Reviewing and setting new expectations is part of everyday working. 'There's more work' is probably a conversation we're very used to having. But how often do we talk about releasing expectations? How often do we deliberately talk – with ourselves or with our team – about what we should stop doing, and what we should ditch to make space for what we've taken on?

 'You can't reach for anything new if your hands are still full of yesterday's junk.'

Louise Smith

But sometimes what we hold on to isn't necessarily junk. It might be the product that sells but isn't particularly profitable. Or the legacy project that's not quite failing but equally not going anywhere fast. Or the campaign or event you've 'always done' that doesn't really line up with your current vision.

> **brilliant tip**
>
> When reviewing your personal or team workload, practise asking this question: What can we release? What can we be ruthless with?

How much of this problem are we creating, contributing towards or reinforcing?

A great shift in perspective happens when the productivity conversation changes from, 'How do we cope with all this relentless work?' to 'How much of this are we creating for ourselves?'

- When one sales team leader speaks up and says, 'Yes, we do spend a lot of our time chasing the 80 per cent instead of focusing on the 20 per cent,' it opens up the conversation and gives permission for the rest of the team to challenge their collective focus.

- When the web designer, whose customers always frustrate her by leaving things to the last minute, realises that with the right conversations and pre-planning she can proactively manage her clients and give them a nudge that does wonders for their own project management – 'Oh thanks for the prompt! I've been meaning to get in touch with you about that' – this helps them as well as with her own planning.

- When the head of department realises that every email he sends generates more inbound traffic, and every time he replies 'out of hours' he reinforces the expectation that he is available out of hours and sets an unintended expectation for the rest of the department too.

What's hampering your productivity or your team's productivity at the moment? How much of it have you created for yourselves, do you contribute to or perpetuate with your own working habits? The beauty of being involved in creating the problem means that you're in a great place to be part of the solution.

What do you want . . . and what do you need from me?

What do you do when you're the person that everybody turns to?

The oracle who knows everything and everyone. The problem solver that everyone wants in their meeting. The natural helper who can always be relied on to help you out of a pickle. The unofficial counsellor – the wise voice of reason who talks you out of hitting someone or gives you a shoulder to cry on. Or the boss people turn to for direction, decisions and authority.

It can be flattering, a real honour to be the person that other people turn to when they need help, but it can also be tricky to be the go-to person when you've also got a lot on your plate.

 **example**

One University Dean found he regularly arrived to a queue outside his office of people who wanted to ask for his expertise, decision, authority or influence. People who wanted him to help them solve a problem. Before he let them through the door, they had to answer two questions:

- What do you want?
- What have you already done about this?

He wanted to make sure that they had already done the ground work – that not only had they clarified the problem, but they also had an outcome in mind – a proposed solution – and had already done what they could do to tackle the problem. It ensured that they were focused on finding a solution, not just there to present a problem. It reminded them to take ownership of finding a solution, rather than just pass the problem onto him. And when the word spread and people knew to expect these questions, they were often pretty clear of exactly what they needed from him by the time they arrived at his office – whether it was his authorisation, his influence, his perspective, his backing or his budget they needed.

It can be quite cathartic to be on the receiving end of these kinds of questions too. I remember calling a colleague for a second opinion on an article I had written for a high-profile publication, and he asked me directly: 'What do you really need from me here? Do you need my professional opinion on how this piece reflects on the company? Or are you just having an insecure author moment?' The question made me laugh out loud. He was spot on: I was indeed having an insecure author moment. What I really needed was just a voice of reassurance – in a moment where I didn't trust my own judgement, I needed someone who knew me well, and who knows my writing well, to tell me what I needed to hear: 'Stop worrying. Trust yourself. It will be fine.' And indeed it was.

Do you have this on your radar?

- 'Rachel, are you going to be updating the brochure?'
- 'Yes, Dave, it's on my long list of things to do but I need to XYZ first.'
- 'OK, I just wanted to know if it was on your radar.'

Not everything that arrives in your inbox is an action. But sometimes it can feel like that. When someone sends you a client to contact, an idea they had for your project, or a piece of information to take into account, it can sometimes feel like they've just given you another piece of work to do. Do they want you to contact them straight away? Do you need to reply? Do you need to report back to them or keep them updated?

To make life easier and avoid ambiguity, make it clear if you are requesting an action: 'Please can you update the brochure and let me know when it's done' or if you are leaving it with them, 'I noticed the brochure needs updating too. Just checking you've got that on your radar as part of your branding project?'

Firefighting like the pros

Sometimes things don't go to plan. Sometimes plans change. Sometimes we have to fight fires. We often associate firefighting with panic, chaos and running around like a headless chicken. But how do the professionals fight fires?

- **With calm and focus.** They assess the situation and deal with it. They know that panic impairs their ability to make the right decisions, so they ensure that their heads are in the right place to respond quickly and effectively.
- **As a team.** Firefighters rarely tackle fires by themselves. They recognise that working as part of a team means that they cover each other's backs and blind spots, provide reinforcement and extra capacity to lighten the load. Communication is vital to ensure everyone is working

together in the same direction, and helping rather than hindering. Who's part of your team? Who can give you that extra perspective, sanity check or an extra hand? What happens when a crisis hits? Do you shut everyone out? Does your team all run around doing their own thing? Or do you pull together to put out the fire?

- **With a plan.** Firefighters always have a plan. They spend time away from the fires working out how best to tackle fires. They do the thinking upfront, so that in the heat of the moment, they already know exactly what they need to do and can spring into action straight away. How much space do you make in your week to clarify your strategy and plans?

- **With protection.** They take care of themselves. They make sure they are fit to fight fires. They take care to ensure they do not compromise their ability to continue fighting fires by putting themselves at risk in one fire.

- **With prevention.** A large part of a firefighter's job is spent educating people and raising awareness to prevent fires. The more fires they can prevent the fewer fires they have to fight, and of course the lower the cost in lives (and resources).

- **With capacity.** Firefighters always take capacity really seriously. Think about it, at any given time you wouldn't want the entire fire brigade out fighting fires, because who's going to deal with the next one? Firefighters make sure they always have the capacity to respond – even if they can't predict when the next fire is going to be.

The importance of margin

How much margin do you give yourself? Most of us tend to fill our calendars to the brim, trying to figure out how to squeeze another five-minute job in between those two meetings. We think that makes us efficient. But let's face it, when we stack the bricks up high, it doesn't take much to topple the tower – a last-minute emergency, a printer error, car trouble, train delay or broadband outage – for a well-planned day to suddenly spiral out of control.

Counter-intuitively, the most powerful productivity tool we can have in our arsenal is margin.

brilliant definition

Margin
The space between our load and our limits.

Margin is having time beyond what is necessary, blank space in the diary that gives us time to deal with the work that over-spills, the unexpected glitches and the emergency fire-fighting. It is breathing space that gives us space to change our minds, choice to stop, time to think, grow, laugh and play. Like air in a pillow, the value of space is in itself immaterial but plays a vital role in between what's solid, to allow for movement and comfort and to absorb impact.

Having margin means that when that lightning bolt of creative genius hits, we can go with it wholeheartedly. It gives us the freedom to be pleasantly interrupted by an opportunity we couldn't have planned for. It gives us the capacity to respond to a cry for help, to receive an unexpected blessing, to be capti-vated by a perfect sunset.

 'So many people are being robbed from a life of meaning, not because they are not committed but because they are over-committed.'

Craig Groeschel[3]

Spare capacity can mean the world. Spare capacity can change the world. What if we had the capacity to stop for just five minutes a day to help someone out: to hold the door, give directions, stop and smile, or tell someone to take their time? Or when someone turns up unexpectedly, to say, 'Pull up a chair and join us', to be patient with the intern who's still learning the ropes, or find out how your new colleague is settling into being in a new town.

How much does your schedule depend on everything running like clockwork? How prepared are you for the unexpected? How much margin do you have for other people's mistakes?

brilliant example

I am a recovering perfectionist. I've always had high standards of myself, but I've never demanded perfection from others. In fact, even when I've been hard on myself, I've still been encouraging others to be kinder on themselves. I'm too 'nice' to be a perfectionist when it comes to other people . . . or so I thought.

It was midnight. I was home from a two-hour drive and I had a workshop the next morning. I thought I had it all worked out: I knew it was going to be a bit of a three-day marathon, I'd scoped ahead, taken a deep breath and gotten everything prepared and lined up in advance. What I didn't plan for was someone else's mistake and oversight, which meant instead of going straight to bed, I found myself doing emergency printing at midnight. Disaster was averted, and even though I had a terrible night's sleep, the workshop went brilliantly.

But it did get me thinking: yes, it was someone else's mistake, yes, they should have spotted it, yes, they could have given themselves more time (it had also been a busy season for them). No, it wasn't my job to make ▶

sure they did theirs, and yes, we would be having a conversation about it. (Thankfully, I knew better than to fire off an email when tired and very grumpy!)

I realised this: when my schedule is so tight that there is no margin for error, then by default I am demanding perfection – not just from me – but from everyone around me.

Creating margin

The thing about margin is we all love the idea. But in reality, in a world where we're already stretched, it seems really really hard to do! The trick is to start small. Here are some ideas:

- Build an extra hour or day into your deadline.
- Leave the office ten minutes early to make that appointment.
- Book in a 30-minute slot for a 20-minute meeting (make sure everyone's aware it's a 20-minute meeting).
- Take one thing off today's to-do list and don't replace it.
- Say no to one meeting or one extra request this week.
- Ask for that file a day earlier than you need it.
- Give yourself a lunch break and leave the phone at your desk when you take it.
- Give yourself an extra ten minutes on top of travel time in between your meetings, so you can gather your thoughts, capture your actions, etc.
- Set your 'out of office' autoreply to tell people you return from holiday one day later than you actually come back, so you can catch up with yourself before everyone wants a piece of you. (Let the people who can see you in your office know that's what you're doing – or work from home.)

Letting others do what they can do

Part of creating margin is letting others do what they can do, so you can do what only you can do. Yes, they might do it slower, or badly to begin with. Yes, it will take time to get them up to speed – so initially it may slow you down too. And no, they probably won't do it the same way as you. To delegate is to entrust. To let go of the fine control and trust someone else to get the job done. The goal is to stop being the bottleneck.

The easiest things to delegate are simple tasks and well-documented processes – worker mode tasks, where you've already defined the parameters of the job, it's just up to someone else to execute. What's harder is where decisions are involved, but even then you can still build in margin, for example:

Many thanks for your email. I have cc'd _____ who would be delighted to run through the options for you and your team, she will be in touch as soon as she is free to help you (please bear in mind that she may be delivering a workshop at the moment though, so may not be able to respond today).

Or for Richard Tubb, an IT business consultant who occasionally gets interview requests from people in far-flung time zones that fall outside of his normal working hours, instead of asking his PA to check with him each time (and making himself the bottleneck) I suggested giving his PA the authorisation to pencil in appointments and set expectations accordingly: 'Richard doesn't normally have appointments on those days/at those times but he will make an exception to accommodate your time zone. Let me pencil you in and confirm once I've checked with him/let you know if that's a problem.'

What about managing up?

- 'I'm pretty good at organising myself, but I don't know what to do with my boss!'
- 'I think I'm on track, then wham – my boss comes out of a meeting and it's all change again!'
- 'Everything's urgent and last minute. How can I plan ahead if my boss doesn't?'

Sometimes the chaos comes from the top. The last-minute boss, the overenthusiastic Tigger, the micromanager or the seagull boss (who flies in, dumps on you, then flies off again).

---

brilliant example

Jenny was at her wits' end with her boss. He would email her ideas off the top of his head, usually with a super tight deadline, she would work hard to deliver what she thought he wanted, only to have him redo everything or change his mind about what he wanted. She was someone who prided herself on getting things right, but it felt like however hard she tried, it was never right with him. In fact, she would often deliver something that worked fine, but by the time he tweaked and fiddled with it, he'd hand it back to her broken. She started questioning herself, her competence and capability, and almost like a self-fulfilling prophecy she started making mistakes in other areas of her work too.

How do you deal with a seagull boss or an overenthusiastic Tigger?

Understand what's happening behind the scenes

When we personalise the situation, we start to think that it's either all our fault, like Jenny did, or all their fault: 'He doesn't care, she's failing to communicate,' or even 'They're doing it on purpose'.

Take a step back and look at the wider picture. What's going on in the wider world? Are you in a season of rapid change? Is your boss reacting to new mandates as much as you are? Do they have a 'seagull boss' firing surprises at them everyday? Are they reacting to a new industry climate or a demanding customer? Are they suffering from new parent sleep deprivation? Or is it part of their personality? Do they naturally tend to think much more in the moment? Are they firing ideas at you at the point where they are forming, rather than when they're fully formed?

When you understand what's happening behind the scenes, you'll have a better understanding of what's motivating your boss or winding them up, be less emotionally affected yourself and shift your perspective from 'Why are you doing this to me?' to 'What's going on and how can I help?' and be in a better place to make decisions that are good for both of you.

Understand what they want from you

Are they clear about what they want from you or are they inviting your input in defining the work? Do they have the bare bones of an idea they want you to add flesh to? Do they have an idea they want you to expand by yourself, or help them explore? Are they saying, 'Build this end product ready to deliver to the client' or, 'Can you put something together along these lines to see what it might look like?' or even, 'Hey, I've got a new idea, can you help me figure out if it's got legs?'

Knowing what they want will help you to avoid putting in hours of fine detail when they only want an overview, or delivering a quick and dirty one-pager when they actually wanted a 50-page report.

 **example**

Jenny thought her boss wanted her to deliver the final product, so every time he changed his mind she felt like she was having to redo work. Whereas as an 'ideas' person, her boss was just asking her to put each stage of his idea into action, so each iteration was actually progress because it helped him to get one step closer to the final goal.

Ask questions to clarify exactly what they want from you, so you don't have to guess – and they get what they want. As a result you won't waste time second guessing, redoing work or running in opposite directions.

Understand their communication style – and yours

If they have a tendency to think out loud, what they say at the beginning may not be the decision they end up with at the end. Make sure you listen to the idea as it unfolds, and check that you've understood the final decision of what they want you to do. Ask if you can email them with a summary of your understanding of what's been agreed – so that you're both clear about what you're working towards, and what your next actions will be.

If you need more time to process what's been said, say that you'd like to digest this further and ask if you can come back to them within a particular timeframe with any questions – or even before you make a decision. If you need a checkpoint halfway through, schedule that in at the beginning: 'Let me put some rough ideas together and send them over. Can we check in on Wednesday to make sure I'm on the right track?'

This way, you don't have to do all your thinking on the spot and you are both free to communicate in your own styles, resulting in fewer misunderstandings and better communication.

Pre-empt, don't mind-read

If your boss has a habit of asking for things last minute, the more you know about their projects and deadlines, the more you can pre-empt and call attention to things that might require your input ahead of time. Use your review or one-to-one meetings to check in both ways – not just to review your performance and workload but also to find out about what's going on in their world. What's their main focus right now? What key projects are they working on? How does your role fit into that?

- 'You're meeting with the client next week. Is there anything you'll be needing from me before then?'
- 'The deadline for submission is at the end of the month. Let me get a draft to you by the 15th, then we can meet on the 17th to review and agree any changes.'
- 'Who else is involved in this project? Do we need to get their input on this too?'
- 'Have you considered . . .?'

When you take the opportunity to scope ahead and have a pro-active conversation with your boss, you can both benefit from less reactive working and fewer surprises.

Use an umbrella

Sometimes when it comes pouring down you do need an umbrella! If you find yourself on the receiving end of a bar-rage of emails, with enthusiastic new ideas, hot-off-the-press requests, or a furious rant, it can be helpful to defer the decision and buy some cooling-off time.

- 'That's a great idea. Let me come back to you.'
- 'Let me get this project out of the door then I'll be able to give this my full attention.'

- 'Lots of great ideas here. Best to talk them over. How about Friday?'
- 'I'll discuss this with . . .'
- 'Let me think this over.'
- 'Let's talk in the morning.'

Listen, acknowledge, then give yourself some breathing space so you respond to the core of the issue with your best answers rather than react to the noise surrounding it.

Offer alternatives

It can be hard to say 'no' outright to your boss. But if what they're asking for is not going to work, or is likely to be costly, it's up to you to communicate that.

- 'I can give you the quick and dirty version today, or the fully polished version next Thursday. Which would you prefer?'
- 'I can get this to you by close of play tomorrow if I put Project X on the back burner. That means we'll have to push back the launch to May. What do you want to do?'
- 'The earliest I can get this to you is Wednesday. What you can use in the meantime is . . .'
- 'What about . . .?'
- 'This is what I can do . . .'

When you communicate your perspective, not only do you negotiate what works best for you, but you also give your boss added clarity of what's doable and what the impact is likely to be. As a result, you develop a common understanding of what the right things are, and more of the right things get done.

 **recap**

You can't control everything, especially when it comes to other people, but you can manage your attention and availability, you can set expectations that make life easier for everyone, you can influence the conversations you have as a team to build better working relationships and more productive team working, and you can create margin that enables you and those around you to do your best work.

References

[1] The Sean Blog, 2011. 'Leave me alone!!! (using Lync to NOT communicate)'. Available at: http://blogs.technet.com/b/seanearp/archive/2011/09/06/leave-me-alone-using-lync-to-not-communicate.aspx

[2] Dr Penny Pullan is founder of Making Projects Work Ltd, which focuses on solutions to make projects and programmes work. Available at: http://makingprojectswork.co.uk

[3] 'Margin' series, LifeChurch.tv. Available at: www.lifechurch.tv/message-archive/watch/margin/2/message/low-res

CHAPTER 6

Setting boundaries and saying no

You can't do everything. And you certainly can't please everyone all of the time. When we try to be everything to everyone, we end up spreading ourselves thin, diluting our impact and winding up exhausted.

But even when you know this, it can still be hard to put it into practice. Setting and maintaining boundaries takes practice, and saying no often requires both diplomacy and assertiveness.

Here are some practical ways of setting healthy boundaries, managing expectations and saying no with grace and confidence.

What are boundaries?

People often struggle to define boundaries because they think boundaries are about keeping people out.

- 'I don't want to say no because I don't want to be rude or unhelpful.'
- 'I don't want to pass up an opportunity in case they never ask again.'
- 'I don't want to tick off my boss.'
- 'We can't ignore our customers!'

You don't want to be rude, ungenerous, or unwelcoming. You don't want to turn clients away or put people off. You don't want to offend or upset. You don't want to put your job or your relationship on the line.

brilliant tip

Boundaries are more about valuing what's inside, than keeping people out.

brilliant definition

Author Danny Silk writes about boundaries in a parenting context, but the same principle applies to our working relationships too:

Boundaries communicate value for what is inside of those boundaries. If you have several junk cars out in a field, it's called an eyesore. If you put a fence around those cars, then you have a wrecking yard. And if you put a building around those cars, you have a garage. With each increase of limits you increase the value of what is inside. When you raise the level of what you require before you will allow access, you increase the value of what you have. To all who are near, we send a clear message about the level of value we have for ourselves by the way we establish boundaries.[1]

To have boundaries you have to value yourself. The boundaries around your personal time and commitments, as well as your family or team's commitments, communicate how much you value yourself, your family and your team.

How valuable is your time and attention? How valuable is your contribution? How valuable are you, your team or your family? How well do your boundaries communicate this?

What happens when you don't set boundaries?

Initially in the short term it might just be an inconvenience – an extra hour here, an extra commitment there, cancelling on one of your own plans, or being out of pocket once. But when it keeps happening, an inconvenience becomes a toleration, and the longer you tolerate something, the more of a toll it takes, and the more established it becomes.

 **reflection**

- 'Tim is always in the office early.'
- 'Sarah's always the last one to leave.'
- 'Kate can always pick up the pieces.'
- 'Mum's never home.'
- 'Dad's always on his phone.'

What would your colleagues, friends or family say about you?

What starts as an exception can become a norm, and your initial reluctance can turn into resentment. You can find yourself feeling powerless, when something you initially chose to let happen becomes something that just happens to you.

No one else can set your boundaries for you. It's up to you to define what you value, and how much you value it. It's up to you to establish the rules of engagement and to set expectations. Just as the walls of a house provide definition, support and security, you'll find that when you do set boundaries they actually strengthen and enhance your relationships, as well as your productivity.

Saying no, so you can say yes

The curse of the capable is that there are lots of things we can do. Even if it's not what we do best, what we enjoy doing best, or what gets the best out of us. The extra project you're asked to be involved in because you have some expertise or experience in that area. The client who's not ideal or the jobs you take on 'just to tide you over'. The tasks that need doing that may not be your field of expertise, but nevertheless need to be done.

We've all done it, and when it enables you to do what you love, and move forward in the right direction, it can have its place. Being flexible and resourceful, being willing to do the hard things is both necessary and noble. But operating outside of your strengths zaps you, and can easily take over your time, energy and headspace, leaving you with no capacity or strength for what you really want to do, what you do best and what energises you. When you settle for what you 'can do' too often, it can leave you feeling resentful, frustrated, unfulfilled or drained.

---

brilliant example

'I wish there weren't so many things that I can do!' My husband said this a little while ago. He was at a crossroads in his career, and was trying to decide which direction he wanted to steer in. His problem was, he was too capable. For most of his career, he had followed his competency – and the money, opportunities and promotion that had come with it – and found himself doing a job he was very good at but didn't enjoy.

'It would be easier if I was only good at one thing!' – because then he wouldn't have to choose.

It's easy to say no to things you know you can't do. It's a whole lot harder to say no to things you know you can do. Things you can turn your hand to, things you can figure out, things that if you tried hard enough you can master pretty well. Things other people might well ask you to do, because they know you'd do a pretty decent job at it. Even things that are easier to do than the work you know you should be doing!

But these things can often take more time to figure out, more energy to complete and give you fleeting satisfaction rather than lasting fulfilment. The problem with being capable is there are far too many things we 'can' do. And when we say yes to all those things, we end up with nothing left to give to the things we truly want to do.

Sometimes we need to say no, not because we can't do it, but because it's not the right thing for us to do. Sometimes we need to let others do what they can do, so we can do what only we can do. So that we can make space. Space for what we do best. Space for what we love. Space, so we can say yes wholeheartedly to what matters to us.

 **reflection**

What do you want to say yes wholeheartedly to? What do you need to say no to, in order to do that?

Stop mind-reading (or expecting others to)

Have you ever found yourself in one of these situations?

- You ask someone if they know of anyone who could help you do something, when really you want them to offer, and they don't get the hint.

- You need to raise a performance issue with a colleague/ member of staff but skirt around the issue. You find yourself saying, 'How was the traffic this morning?' and, 'Is everything OK?', and then you accept a vague answer that leaves you none the wiser why they're often 15–30 minutes late for key meetings.

● Someone who's come into your office for a chat outstays their welcome. You make hints about how busy you are, and keep looking at your screen hoping they get the message, but they just keep talking.

Sometimes we find it hard to say what we really mean, so we drop hints and might even try to 'sell' a more attractive alternative instead of asking for what we really need. The problem with this is it involves mind-reading and can often leave us feeling frustrated or even resentful.

Instead of trying to pre-empt, hint or mind-read, ask for what you need:

● 'I need some help with this project – do you have capacity to take on an extra client right now?'

● 'Is there any reason why you're often 15–30 minutes late for key meetings?'

● 'I need to dive into this report now, but I'm free at lunchtime if you need some help figuring that one out.'

When you ask for what you need, and ask others what they need, you can come up with a solution together. No more mind-reading!

Challenge your defaults

Do you find yourself being the default go-to person at work or at home? Here are some common examples:

● **The default oracle:** the one who knows everything and everyone. The one people come to before they ask Google,

Wiki, the Intranet or the person who's actually responsible for answering that question.

- **The default fixer:** the natural problem solver who's the first port of call when the stuff hits the fan. The one who gets asked, 'Could you take a look at this?', even when it's completely outside their area.

- **The default organiser:** the one who takes the drinks order when you all rock up at a café, and has probably phoned ahead, booked the table in the corner and checked if there's soya milk for the dairy intolerant person. The one everyone else turns to and asks, 'What's the plan?'.

- **The default decision maker:** the one who gets copied in on emails with 'What do you think?' and invited to meetings 'because we value your opinion'.

- **The default emergency hero:** the one who you can always get hold of at the last minute, who you can rely upon to jump into action at the drop of the hat.

- **The default counsellor:** the first person people turn to when they need a shoulder to cry on or a sounding board to rant at. The one who knows about all the make-ups and break-ups in the office, the hospital visits and whose kids are teething.

- **The default perfecter:** one person I worked with recently said that her perfectionism became so well known within her team, that someone she delegated to actually delivered the piece of work to her with the words: 'It's not quite there yet but I know you'll check it through and make it right.'

 **reflection**

Which of these do you recognise in yourself?

We choose our defaults, however much it feels the other way. Sometimes deliberately, because actually we quite like being that person. Sometime because we made a decision once upon a time, when it made perfect sense, and haven't questioned it since. And sometimes just out of habit.

It's good to revisit our defaults from time to time, and to ask how well they're working for us, and if they are still relevant and helpful – especially if your role, remit or circumstances have changed.

How do you stop being the default person – if you choose to?

Make yourself less available

People will always default to the quickest or easiest route, so making it harder to find it from you can make all the other options much more attractive. Delay responding, be less accommodating, say no from time to time. Point them in the right direction even if it takes just as much time as giving them the answer or doing it for them. Give them an incentive to go find the answer by a different means.

Hand over the responsibility

'You decide, I trust you.' Yes, it may be quicker to make the decision for them, but this way you're training them to let go of defaulting to you and get used to making their own decisions.

Accept it takes time to learn

If you've been doing something day in, day out for 12 years, someone who's just getting started won't be as quick or as efficient, and most likely won't do it the same way as you either. Step aside. Give them space and time to learn, and let them develop their own way of doing things.

Let it go

As well as letting go of control, we also need to let go of being needed. Let's face it, it feels good to be in demand, and sometimes that's the hardest part to let go of. But we can't fully step into our present role, if we've always got one foot trapped in the past.

Leading those you serve

We often think that serving means to let someone else take the lead, and to respond or react as appropriate. Whether that's customer service, serving our community, our boss or our family members. We ask them what they want and we endeavour to give it to them.

But that places a certain responsibility on the person we're serving. To know what's possible. To know what's appropriate. If you walked into a restaurant of a certain calibre, you'd expect the waiter to guide you to a table, give you a menu, tell you if anything's not available that day, maybe give you some recommendations or specials of the day, and ask you what you'd like to drink. Yes, if you asked for a different table, or an alternative side dish, they would also respond to that. But if they simply said 'What do you want?' when you arrived, that would be pretty hard work for you as the customer, let alone the waiter and the chef!

---

brilliant example

I have a local taxi company who are very reliable. Their prices are consistent, their drivers are always on time and they don't dawdle to rack up the meter. By all accounts they offer excellent service. Until something goes wrong. I'd ▶

once ordered a taxi to pick me up from the train station at 11.30 pm. The train had already been delayed when I called, so I explained that I hoped to be at the station for that time. As it happened, I was delayed by a further ten minutes. By the time I arrived at the station, there was no taxi in sight. I called the company.

> 'Well, you booked it for 11:30, when you didn't show the driver left.'
>
> 'OK, but my train was delayed . . .'
>
> 'You could have called us . . .'
>
> 'True, but the signal on the train isn't great – plus I already told you it was already running late.'
>
> 'We had no way of knowing if you were coming, the driver can't afford to wait around for no shows.'
>
> 'You knew I was on a train . . . there's not much of a chance I'm not going to show is there?'
>
> 'Well, I can send him back.'
>
> 'How long will that be?'
>
> 'Ten minutes.'
>
> 'Never mind, I can see there's a taxi at the rank. I'll take that instead.'
>
> 'So you're saying you don't want a taxi now.'
>
> 'Yes.'
>
> 'Fine.' Hangs up.

Well, that was a pretty poor outcome for both of us. The driver and the company lost out on a fare. As the customer I felt let down. Nobody wins.

What's interesting about this conversation is that nothing the taxi company did was *wrong* as such. But the way in which they did it left them out of pocket and the customer feeling let down. They were enforcing boundaries which were pretty fair, but hadn't been communicated. And when questioned, their response was defensive, which of course got my back up too.

Here's what they could have done differently:

- **Set clear expectations about delays:** 'Our drivers will wait for five minutes max. If you're delayed longer than that you need to let us know.'

- **Acknowledge the dilemma:** 'I'm sorry about that. Our drivers can only wait for five minutes as we often get no shows. What I can do is send someone back. They'll be there in ten minutes. Would you like me to do that?'

- **Offer a better solution for the future:** 'Listen, next time, give us a call when you're ten minutes away. That way we'll be able to get a taxi to you by the time you arrive and there's less chance of your train being delayed at that point.'

Setting the boundary upfront would have also prompted me to offer to pay for waiting time, which I'd have been happy to do (I don't want the driver to be out of pocket, but I'd rather not be a lone female hanging around a train station at that time of night). They could have said yes or no to that, but at least I would know exactly what to expect.

How often do you feel aggrieved when your boundaries are crossed? How clearly have you communicated them? How much have you assumed that they will know? How much do you lead your customer and set their expectations, or do you leave it up to them to second guess and mind-read?

Sometimes we serve best when we take the lead. When we define what we have to offer and how we work best. When we do the hard work of working out the best way of meeting our customers' needs. When we set clear expectations up front, and guide the customer through the experience.

- I serve my children when I offer them a balanced meal – rather than asking them what they want (chocolate, chocolate and more chocolate).
- I serve my clients when I let them know my working hours and availability.
- I serve my colleagues when I tell them I can give my best answer on Friday rather than a rushed and hurried one now.
- I serve my boss when I tell him that I don't have the capacity to give that project the attention it deserves.
- I serve my family when I ask for help with the laundry rather than huff and puff with resentment that I have to do everything myself.

⤢ brilliant reflection

How can you serve your people better, by taking a lead, defining boundaries and setting clear expectations?

How you work best

If you're a designer who works best when you get a feel for your client's passion, style and personality – and are much more inspired by an intimate chat over coffee than a detailed project brief – then tell them that. If on the other hand you need a structured brief to work from and your client is notoriously bad at providing detail, then acknowledge that there's a translation job to be done first: 'I'm going to email you with a summary of what we've agreed. What I'd like you to do is to reply and confirm I've captured everything accurately before I start working on it.'

If you prefer to digest things internally and give your best input when you've had time to think, ask your clients to email you their ideas or an agenda before the meeting, so you can be prepared. Let them know that's how you work best. If they surprise you with an idea, don't be flustered, accept it with the enthusiasm it was offered, and buy yourself time by saying, 'Let me think on that and come back to you.'

On the other hand, if you think best on your feet and in conversation, then reply to the email with, 'Let's talk about this. I'd like to understand a bit more about . . . How's Friday for you?'

If you like to have the whole picture before you begin, then ask for it. Explain that once you know what you're doing you'll go away, get it done and come back to them with everything complete. If on the other hand you prefer a step-by-step approach and prefer to get feedback along the way, agree some checkpoints in advance.

If you're holding dates for someone, how long will you hold them for?

brilliant example

I once spent a week holding one opportunity at bay while I checked if someone else still wanted a date they had asked me to hold a few weeks ago. I couldn't get hold of them in the end and had to release the date. It was time consuming and frustrating for me and I worried about disappointing the first client. Graham reminded me that we have a policy for this reason, of holding dates for one week, and when we are clear about this upfront, clients benefit from the certainty of having their dates on hold for a week, and know that if they took longer than a week, those dates would get released and may be booked by someone else.

⤴ brilliant reflection

How do you work best? How often will you check in? What's the best way to keep in touch in between meetings? What if things change?

Addressing some of these questions upfront not only makes life easier for you, but also gives others more certainty in dealing with you.

What happens next?

'What happens next?' is a question that your clients, colleagues or boss might have. Instead of waiting for them to ask, and potentially interrupting you when your focus is elsewhere, take the opportunity to clarify this up front, so they (and you) know what to expect.

▶ brilliant example

Here's how printing company MOO (moo.com) uses their confirmation emails to proactively set customer expectations and communicate what happens next:

Hello _____

I'm Little MOO – the bit of software that will be managing your order with moo.com. It will shortly be sent to Big MOO, our print machine who will print it for you in the next few days. I'll let you know when it's done and on its way to you.

If you've imported your images to MOO from another site, please make sure you don't remove or change the photos you've chosen from that site until this order has been printed, or some pictures may come out blank.

(If you've uploaded them directly to MOO, then there's no need to worry.)

You can track and manage your order from the accounts section at: https://secure.moo.com/account

Estimated arrival date: Mon 11 May 2015

Remember, I'm just a bit of software. So, if you have any questions regarding your order please first read our Frequently Asked Questions at: http://www.moo.com/help/faq/ and if you're still not sure, contact Customer Service (who are real people):

By email/online chat:

http://www.moo.com/help/contact-us.html

By phone:

UK: 0207 392 2780 – 9.30am–10pm BST Mon–Fri (excl. public holidays)

Thanks,
Little MOO, Print Robot

What if my boundaries have already been crossed?

It's one thing setting boundaries, but what happens if you've already allowed your boundaries to be crossed, or if you haven't been clear enough in setting them in the first place?

- 'People are used to me being available after hours.'
- 'I've already said yes when I should have said no!'
- 'I said yes to fill the gap in the short term, but fast-forward nine months and there's an unspoken assumption that I'll carry on filling in the gap. I'm feeling a bit taken advantage of . . .'

When your boundaries have already been crossed it can be a bit tricky to extricate yourself. If you've promised to deliver you may not be able to pull out immediately or entirely. If you've

set an expectation it may take time to change that expectation
and there may be some diplomatic retraining needed and some
comfort zone stretching for you.

- **Take small steps:** 'I'm in the Welsh mountains this weekend
  so probably going to be offline, so if anything comes up just
  drop them over by email and I'll pick it up on Monday.'
- **Find opportunities to revisit and redefine boundaries:**
  - 'We've been working together for six months now, it
    would be really good to review how this is working.'
  - 'This project has really taken off – it's approaching
    the point where it's going to need full-time dedicated
    support. Let's talk about how we transition to that?'
  - 'I've taken a deeper look and I think it's actually going
    to require a lot more than I initially thought. I don't have
    the time/expertise to do it justice right now. I'd love to
    support you in a different way though. How about . . .'
- **Refer to the common outcome you share:** 'Our customers
  need to feel valued for sure. I'm wondering if there's a
  better way to achieve this? Can I run some ideas past you?'
- **Help others to set boundaries:** 'Listen, I'm on call this
  weekend so you might get some emails from me – I don't
  need you to look at them or take any action until you're
  back in the office, OK?'
- Ask for help.

---

brilliant example

One workshop delegate I worked with once admitted that she found it really
hard to say 'no'. Her boss was in the room and said, 'Thank you for saying
that - that's really good to know, because I go to meetings and say "yes" to
more work for our team because I think you have the capacity. Now that I
know that's not necessarily the case, I can take that into account!'

Sometimes when we're used to having our boundaries crossed (or not setting them in the first place), we may not be very used to asserting our own value and the validity of our boundaries. Others around you may see your value much more clearly than you can, and can support you in setting and resetting your boundaries.

Embracing imperfection and learning from mistakes

From an early age I could tell my kids had different ways of dealing with mistakes. One would spot a tiny mistake and want to fix it straight away. The other would try and sweep it under the carpet (sometimes literally) and try not to deal with it.

Mistakes are uncomfortable, but the more we hide them the more they tend to grow and fester. Overlooking them doesn't make them go away. If anything, it creates a breeding ground for more mistakes. But equally, turning it into a witch hunt creates a culture of shame and blame which naturally makes us want to hide even more.

A friend of mine once had a boss whose mantra about mistakes was: 'I don't care if you f*** up, as long as you own up and clear up.' What I love about this is that it tells us two things:

1 Mistakes are not the end. There is life after a mistake and what matters is what we do next.
2 It also separates the person making the mistake from the mistake itself.

The mistake is the problem. The person needs to be part of the solution. When we define ourselves by our mistakes, we can end up pouring our energies into defending, hiding or justifying our mistakes – or identifying ourselves as the failure or problem. Yes, mistakes happen, and yes, there's often a cost attached to it. But it's also an essential part of learning. Whether that's one person learning a new job, or a whole company learning a new territory.

---

brilliant example

When I was teaching my son to ride his bike, every time he fell off, I knew he needed to get back on, and every time he got back on he got a bit better. Falling off still hurt, but what choice did he have? Avoid the bike, avoid the hurt and give up altogether: failure wins. Ignore the hurt, get back on the bike, hoping he wouldn't fall off again: go into denial. The third choice was to learn to fall well: ditch the bike before you hit the ground, minimising the damage, practise on softer ground, wear protective clothing, for example. Failure sucks. It hurts, it costs, it feels bad. But if we can't avoid it, or ignore it, perhaps we can learn to fail well.

What does failing well look like? Let's start with what it doesn't look like. It doesn't look like what psychologist Henry Cloud describes as the 3Ps of learned helplessness:[2]

Imagine something bad happens: a sales call goes wrong, that product launch fails, a major client is unhappy, or the date night turns into an almighty row. This is what a lot of us do in response:

1 **Make it Personal:** 'It's my fault. I'm not good enough. I am a failure.'

2 **Make it Pervasive:** 'It's not just this one call. It's every call. Nobody wants to buy from me. Nothing I do works. Everything sucks.'

3 **Make it Permanent:** 'It's always like this. Nothing ever works. It will always be this way. All the time.'

Yes, failure hurts, but it hurts a whole lot more when we make it personal, pervasive and permanent. What's more, doing it this way strips away the very traits and resources – our belief, our courage, our vision, tenacity and hope – to recover from our mistakes and fix the problem.

How to do it instead? Instead of the 3Ps, consider these 3Cs:

1 **Clarity:** Henry Cloud calls this Log and Dispute. Log down everything you find yourself thinking about the event itself and what that means. Log down the personal, pervasive and permanent, and challenge those assumptions, e.g.

   ● One person didn't like what you did. What was it they didn't like exactly? What can you do about that? What do you want to do about that? Is it a failing by their measure or yours?

   ● One conversation went wrong. What actually happened? What words were said in what way? What impact did they have? What else was going on at the time?

   ● Was it really a stupid mistake or just a simple mistake? How did it happen? What else was going on at the same time? What simple solution could you put in place to check for these simple mistakes in the future?

2 **Control:** Learned helplessness starts when something happens outside of your control. The way to counter this is to recognise where you can take control. Just as we looked at the circles of influence and concern in Chapter 1, make sure you focus your energy on what you can control or influence, rather than what you can't.

   Looking at a mistake: what factors were at play that led to that mistake? What could you have controlled, what was beyond your control? What can you do now to fix things?

What can you do differently next time? How can you increase your response-ability in the future?

3   **Connection:** Henry Cloud says: 'The human brain survives on three things: oxygen, glucose and relationships.' When we connect with others our perspectives change. We find new solutions to old problems and new strength to fight ongoing battles.

Falling off a bike hurts, yes, but is far more painful if you have to do it on your own. Having support, accountability, encouragement, someone to cheer you on, help you back up, empathise with your pain and rally you back on the bike – that makes the biggest difference.

But it has to be the right people. Falling off a bike in front of someone who just laughs, criticises, belittles or blames you would be worse than doing it on your own. As social researcher Brené Brown, author of *Daring Greatly,* helpfully defines, 'Feedback is sitting on the same side of the table and looking at the issue together.' Not sitting opposite someone with the problem between you. How could you change how you look at mistakes differently? By seeking true feedback. Asking someone to sit at the same side of the table as you to help you to 'fess up and fix it.[3]

brilliant tip

How can you change how you or your team responds to mistakes? By creating a safe environment to 'fess up'. By being more interested in understanding mistakes and finding solutions than apportioning blame. And by giving feedback in a way that says: It's not about me against you. You're not the problem. Your mistake/behaviour/ obstacle is. Let's look at that together.

How to say no

Do you sometimes find yourself saying 'yes' when you really mean to say 'no'? Perhaps it's that really juicy opportunity or the bright shiny new idea that's luring you off track. Or maybe a scary boss, a demanding client or a Very Important Person has put you on the spot. Perhaps like me you're a natural helper who finds it hard to say no because you hate letting people down. Or maybe you're worried that if you say no, they'll never ask again.

Saying 'no' is a skill most of us have to practise. There are a rare few who find it comes naturally to them: 'No. It's just a word. What's the big deal?' For the rest of us, there comes a point where we realise that if we want to be able to choose what we say 'yes' to, we need to learn how to say 'no' comfortably, authentically, pleasantly and effectively. So here are some examples to help.

When you want to say 'not right now'

Yes, you want to help but no, not right now. Right now, you're in the middle of drafting a delicate email, you've already got someone else breathing down your neck, a report deadline that's looming at 12 o'clock, and a meeting that starts in ten minutes. It's not that you don't care or don't want to help, it's just really bad timing, so if 'No, I can't right now' feels rude, abrupt or inappropriate, try saying 'yes' on your own terms:

- 'Yes, I'd love to hear about that. Can we talk at 4?'
- 'Yes, I'm available tomorrow at 10 and at 3 – which would you prefer?'
- 'Yes, let's explore this properly – can we set up a meeting?'

- 'You know what, I'd love to give that some proper thought. Could you email me the details so I can take a closer look?'
- 'Yes, I'd love to help. Given my schedule, the earliest I can come back to you is . . . Would that work, or do you want to find someone else?'

When it's a 'not this time'

So it's an event, opportunity or favour you'd normally welcome, but this time, it's not right for you – for whatever reason. I've just had plenty of these when asking for early reviewers for this book, so here are a few of my favourites:

- 'Sounds great. Sadly I have to practise my ruthlessness on this one and say no. I'd love to, but I'm full up at the moment.'
- 'I love to read – especially your writing – but won't be able to meet the deadline.'
- 'The timing won't work for me this time . . . do please keep me in mind for future feedback.'

When you want to be supportive in a different way

Some of the best 'no' emails I've received are ones where people are genuinely encouraging:

- 'This sounds like a great opportunity and I'm so pleased for you. I'm fully committed with my current projects/ speaking schedule/clients, but I'd love to support you by [introducing you to someone who can help/giving you a resource/promoting the project in a different way].'

When it's a 'thanks but no thanks'

- 'Thanks so much for thinking of me. That's not really my area of expertise but I can recommend . . .'
- 'That's very kind but I'm going to have to decline.'

- 'To be honest, this isn't really my thing. You'd be much better getting _____ on board. Do you want me to introduce you?'
- 'I'm going to pass on this one – but thanks for asking!'

Instead of 'I can't', say 'I don't'

As we looked at in Chapter 2, 'I can't' signals impossibility and incapacity. It makes us feel powerless. Instead 'I don't' sends a different signal to our brains. Whether we say it out loud or just to ourselves, it reminds us that we choose what we commit to, and it feels good to honour our internal commitments:

- 'I don't access my emails at the weekend.'
- 'I don't specialise in that area.'
- 'I don't take calls in the evening.'
- 'I don't travel more than twice a month.'
- 'I don't take on work where I can't give my best, because that doesn't serve anyone.' (OK, that had both 'I don't' and 'I can't' in, but you get the idea . . .)

When you need to enforce boundaries

- 'In order to honour our existing client commitments . . .'
- 'I'm afraid that's only available for _____, but I can point you to this resource which will help you get started . . .'
- 'Our team is fully committed for the next _____, but we do have availability from July onwards.'
- 'I've promised myself no new projects until this one is launched, and now that I've told you I have to stick to it!'
- 'Our training/advertising budget is fully committed for this month/quarter/year. Ask me again in . . .'

'I would love to help you out, but I already made commitments to other _____ (coworkers, clients, etc.) to complete their projects today. It wouldn't be fair to them to not follow through on what I said I would do. I will be sure to fit this in as soon as possible. Thanks for your understanding.'

Elizabeth Grace Saunders[4]

 'Thanks for your interest in meeting with me. Unfortunately, that will not be possible for the foreseeable future. In order to honor my existing commitments, I must decline many worthy invitations like yours.'

Michael Hyatt[5]

 brilliant example

'Ah, that's an intriguing possibility, but I'm afraid that my own Ninja rules of life don't permit working on the weekends. Plus, I doubt the delegates would thank me/us for stealing a possible day of rest from them given how hard the team is working right now. Hope that's OK, I was very tempted to say yes given your keenness to get us in ASAP – but I need to stay authentic to my own Ninja principles!' This was my Ninja colleague Lee's response to a request to run a weekend workshop for a team who couldn't find time in the week to fit in training. They did eventually come back to order, many months later, and the sessions were delivered in work hours, on weekdays.

When you're totally not interested

Do you find conversations with door-to-door sales people, street fundraisers and cold callers annoying and awkward? Here's an idea: use them as an opportunity to practice saying 'no'!

- 'Thanks for asking. This one's not for me, but good luck!'
- 'My regular giving budget is fully committed already.'
- 'I haven't got any advertising budget at all I'm afraid, but thanks for asking!'
- 'We're really not going to have a conservatory. Please don't waste your time with us.'
- 'Love your energy, but it's not for me, thanks!'

Consider this: giving a straightforward 'no' or 'talk to me in x months' time' can actually be more helpful to someone than a vague answer that keeps them guessing.

- 'It's not on the cards I'm afraid. If something changes I'll let you know. Leave it with me.'
- 'It's gone on the back burner but still definitely interested. Ask me again in two months.'
- 'I'm still waiting on . . . hope to have an answer by . . . / check with me again next week.'

Practice

Saying 'no' is a bit like a muscle. It can feel uncomfortable if you haven't used it for a while, but the more you use it, the easier it gets, and the more you realise the world really doesn't end when you do. I've also realised that I'd much rather be asked and given the opportunity (and freedom) to say no, than not to be asked at all. When I feel free to say 'no', then others are free to ask – which means the times when I want to say yes, I can do so wholeheartedly.

 recap

Healthy boundaries clarify what you value and ensure that you have space for what matters most. In fact, it's only when we stop saying yes to everything and start taking the lead, challenging our defaults and clarifying how we work best, that we make a bigger difference, a deeper impact, do better work and deliver more meaningful results in all aspects of our life.

References

[1] Silk, D., Loving Our Kids On Purpose. Available at: http://www
.lovingonpurpose.com/parenting/

[2] Dr Henry Cloud is a clinical psychologist, acclaimed leadership expert and best-selling author. Available at: http://drcloud.com

[3] Brown, B., 2012. *Daring Greatly: How the Courage to Be Vulnerable Transforms the Way We Live, Love, Parent, and Lead.* Penguin: London.

[4] Saunders, E. G., 'Setting boundaries & saying no . . . nicely'. Available at: http://99u.com/articles/7076/setting-boundaries-saying-no-nicely

[5] Hyatt, M., 'Using email templates to say "no" with grace'. Available at: http://michaelhyatt.com/using-email-templates-to-say-"no"-with-grace.html

CHAPTER 7

Understanding your personal productivity style

Productivity is inherently personal. What works for one person won't work in the same way for another. Some would say the secret to productivity is to be super organised while others say it's more about getting into the flow of your passion and creativity. Some say stop talking and get on with it, while others argue that thoughtful and consistent action wins every time.

There's probably a little bit of truth in all those statements for everyone, but we each have our own bias, preference and natural style.

This chapter will help you to identify your own personality and preferences, and tailor your working habits to bring out your best work. It will also show you how to understand those you work with, and provides proven techniques for play to each other's strengths, rather than add to each other's frustrations.

Personality and preferences

The more we understand our own personality and preferences, the more we can tailor our productivity habits and strategies to suit – rather than try and have a personality transplant. One tool I find really useful with clients is the DiSC profile.

DiSC is a behavioural assessment profile which helps you to understand yourself and the people you work with. It gives you insight into your working preferences and tendencies, your motivators and stressors, your needs, communication styles and how to work effectively with people who are different from you, or people who are too much like you. What follows is a brief introduction to the model, to give you an idea of how different behavioural styles give rise to different productivity strengths, challenges and strategies.

Meet Tim, Claudia, Sam and Kate. They are not real people, but rather a representation of different styles, needs and preferences. As you read through their examples, you might find yourself identifying strongly with one or with a blend of characters. Notice what resonates with you – and what insights you can draw out for yourself, and also notice what rings true for other people you work with – your team, your clients, your colleagues, your boss or even members of your family – and ask yourself what this might mean for how you work and relate to them.

D for Dominance

Meet Tim. Tim is bold, ambitious and driven. He loves a challenge and is always the one to push for new horizons and stretch goals. If you want to get something done quick, Tim's your man. He will cut to the chase, have the wheels in motion quicker than you can say 'let's have a meeting'.

His colleagues love his confidence and drive. He's a force of nature; straight to the point and not afraid to speak his mind. Great to have on your side, but woe betide the person who gets in his way. His single-minded focus always gets results, but can be hard for others to keep up with and can sometimes cause collateral damage or land him in hot water.

He's a doer who doesn't have time for indecisiveness and gets bored by the mundane and routine. He hates being bogged down by red tape and protocol. His directness can sometimes come across as rude, and his impatience can make him dismissive of slower or indecisive people. But if you want to get something done quick, or to confront the elephant in the room, he's your man.

If you have a similar style to Tim, make sure you cater for:

● **your natural motivators:** you enjoy initiating change, taking risks, thinking big and being bold, taking charge

brilliant tip

Make sure you have plenty of clear actions and immediate results to focus on, are being challenged by stretching goals and healthy competition and have a good dose of freedom and independence to make your own decisions.

● **your likely procrastination triggers:** too much detail, mundane and routine tasks

brilliant tip

Look for opportunities to delegate/automate or create a challenge by turning it into a game to see how fast you can get them done.

● **your biggest fears:** these are likely to come from losing control, being taken advantage of, or feeling vulnerable

brilliant tip

Watch out for your lizard brain when you feel threatened in these areas.

- **what comes naturally to you:** being decisive, taking charge, casting bold vision and speaking up when nobody else will

> **brilliant** tip
>
> Offer these skills to your colleagues – not everyone finds this easy!

- **what frustrates you:** indecisiveness and having to slow down.

> **brilliant** tip
>
> Avoid long-winded meetings and having nothing to do when you have to wait. Give others the opportunity to think ahead or processing time afterwards. Agree timings and dates so you can park it in @waiting and get on with something else. Offer to join meetings later when the details have been hacked out and a decision is ready to be made.

What to tell your colleagues:

- 'I need the big picture – just give me the headlines.'
- 'Don't worry about sugar coating, you can get straight to the point with me.'
- 'I need to know why we're doing this – what does success look like here? What's the outcome?'
- 'Bear with me, I can be very direct. Excuse me if I come across as blunt. I don't mean to be rude.'
- 'I tend to move quickly and think on my feet. Let me know if I'm going too fast and you need more time to process.'
- 'If I've upset you please tell me.'

I for Influence

Meet Claudia. Claudia is outgoing, enthusiastic and optimistic. A real people person, Claudia comes alive when she's around people – whether that's networking in a room full of strangers, collaborating on projects or having a good natter with friends.

Her colleagues love her passion and energy. A natural story-teller and networker, she can both charm and inspire audiences of all sizes, which is why she's likely to be one of the most well-connected people they know. Her enthusiasm is infectious and brings life to any meeting or party, although sometimes her tendency to gloss over detail can come across as 'fluffy'. An eternal optimist she likes to see possibility in every idea and tends to trust and look for the best in people, which makes her more cautious colleagues nervous.

Impulsive and creative, she prefers to go with the flow. While she is quite happy to fly by the seat of her pants, this can cause chaos for those who prefer a little more stability and preparation and earn her a reputation for being a bit flakey and last minute. Although she wishes she was more organised, she does secretly like the buzz of a deadline. In fact, when there isn't a deadline in sight, she might run out of steam and be distracted by the next shiny thing before she's had a chance to follow through.

If you have a similar style to Claudia, make sure you cater for:

● **your natural motivators:** you enjoy the buzz of new ideas, working with others, expressing yourself and being on the move

brilliant tip

Look for opportunities to talk through your ideas, collaborate, focus on forward movement and express your goals as inspiring positive outcomes rather than problems or pain you want to avoid and build in plenty of opportunity for positive external feedback.

- **your likely procrastination triggers:** too much detail, structure, systematic tasks and too much time alone

brilliant tip

Seek an accountability partner, a change of scenery or look for creative ways to spice up the boring work – and get moving. Your energy comes from being on the move so if you find yourself stuck in a rut, do something (anything) that gets you started.

- **your biggest fears:** these are likely to be around social rejection, disapproval, loss of influence and being ignored

brilliant tip

Watch out for your lizard brain when you feel threatened in these areas.

- **what comes naturally to you:** socialising, networking, encouraging, brainstorming and inspiring

brilliant tip

These are skills you enjoy using and probably find fun and energising, so let your colleagues know that you'd welcome the opportunity to use them!

- **what frustrates you:** critical questions and you shy away from giving unpleasant feedback – you see this as being negative.

brilliant tip

Be aware that sometimes other colleagues may simply have a more naturally 'questioning' style and may not be directly attacking you or your ideas – and sometimes colleagues appreciate you being direct with them. Look for where others are passionate – they might be more reserved or quieter in expressing it, but seeing their passion will help you to get inspired.

What to tell your colleagues:

- 'Can I give you the broad idea and ask you to flesh out the detail?'
- 'What else do you need to know?'
- 'I love a good brainstorm. I'm here if you want to talk it through.'
- 'I think best in conversation – can we have a chat about this?'
- 'Am I getting carried away here? Is there anything I've missed?'
- 'Please feel free to nudge me in a couple of weeks if you haven't heard from me.'
- 'I'd like your feedback – what do you like, what are you not so keen about, and what questions do you have?'

S for Steadiness

Meet Sam. Sam is thoughtful, friendly and patient. A natural helper, Sam loves being part of a team and meeting other people's needs.

His colleagues love his calm, collaborative and supportive nature. He's a true team player, a genuine nice guy and some would say the glue that holds everyone together. He takes a steady, methodical and thorough approach to his work and can always be relied upon to see a job through to completion, but can sometimes frustrates others who want to move forward at a quicker pace. Not one for the limelight, he much prefers to be in the background, refining systems and making everything run smoothly but he does appreciate genuine praise and knowing that he's making a difference.

Because he gets a lot of satisfaction from helping others, he's incredibly accommodating, and will often put other people's needs above his own. He shies away from conflict, so may not always speak his mind, especially if more expressive characters have the floor. He values consensus and collaboration over speed, which can sometimes lead to indecisiveness. His natural empathy combined with his patience makes him a great listener, and an incredibly loyal asset to the team. He's the one who remembers everyone's birthdays, and always goes the extra mile to make sure a customer's totally satisfied.

If you have a similar style to Sam, make sure you cater for:

● **your natural motivators:** you enjoy collaboration, helping people, giving support, and working to a steady rhythm

brilliant tip

Break big goals into steady steps, build in routines that give you stability, seek opportunities to collaborate, develop relationships, focus on how your work supports others, ask for feedback and make sure you have a support network too.

● **your likely procrastination triggers:** conflict, too much task-focused work rather than people-focused work, having to make major decisions independently

brilliant tip

Seek opportunities to collaborate, engage your customers or stakeholders so you can be motivated by the people that you're helping, ask for help to talk through and break down major decisions. Watch out for burnout and being overstretched – build in 'me' time to make sure you are tending to your own needs.

● **your biggest fears:** these are likely to be around loss of stability, change, loss of harmony and offending others

brilliant tip

Watch out for your lizard brain when you feel threatened in these areas.

● **what comes naturally to you:** establishing routines and habits, systemising and making things methodical, breaking big goals into step-by-step actions, bringing a team together, getting people to collaborate, listening, bringing calm to chaos

brilliant tip

You probably do all this so naturally you don't even acknowledge it as a strength, but not everyone finds it easy, so give yourself permission to shine in these areas and take pride in your natural talents.

- **what frustrates you:** decisions that overlook people, working in a tense or chaotic environment, being rushed and reacting to last-minute changes.

brilliant tip

Ask for thinking time to process and build in routines and rhythms to give yourself some certainty, especially if you're in a season of rapid change. Remember that chaos or conflict is not always 'negative' or personal, give people room to rant and blow off steam and know that sometimes the best teams do not always have to agree to be able to work together. If you're making a case for 'people' to someone who is task/results focused, get them on board by drawing the focus back to how it affects bottom line results.

What to tell your colleagues:

- 'This is becoming a regular thing, shall I create a process to make everyone's life easier?'
- 'I'd like to process this a bit further – can I drop you a line later with some more ideas/questions?'
- 'I like to be prepared – can you send me an agenda so I can make sure I come with my best ideas?'
- 'Can we have a quick catch up next week to make sure I'm on the right track?'
- 'Can I send you the draft to make sure I'm on the right track?'
- 'How urgent is this?/When do you need to know by?' (so you can prepare rather than react)
- 'This is happening quicker than I'd like. Can we establish what we need to cut down to accommodate the new deadline?'

C for Conscientiousness

Meet Kate. Kate is quiet, logical and precise. An expert with high standards, Kate loves solving problems and diving deep into detail.

Her colleagues love her thorough eye for detail, and attention to quality. She likes to plan ahead and take a systematic approach to her work, and will persevere with quiet diligence until the job's done. Objective and logical, she much prefers facts to emotion and analysis to assumption and research to impulse. If she doesn't know the answer, she'd rather take her time to figure it out than bluff her way through or go with general consensus.

A true professional, working within strict rules and guidelines don't phase her. In fact, she prefers knowing where she stands, and welcomes the opportunity to bring order and stability with routines and procedures. In social situations she tends to be more private and reserved, seeing little value in casual small talk, but she's not afraid to ask the difficult questions, especially when it comes to analysing risk. In fact, her 101 questions can drive her colleagues mad, especially when they want to move forward quickly, but if you want something done right, you know Kate will leave no stone unturned and no 'i' undotted.

Her focus on high quality and efficiency means she often picks up on details where others glaze over, but as a perfectionist, she reserves her highest standards for herself. She hates being wrong and beats herself up for making mistakes, and is likely to spend much more time preparing, analysing and checking her work compared to others. While this generally pushes her to achieve her best, it can also hold her back from taking risks or taking action until she is 100 per cent certain of her own abilities and the situation in hand.

If you have a similar style to Kate, make sure you cater for:

● **your natural motivators:** enjoy research, analysis, complex details and in-depth problem solving

brilliant tip

Look for opportunities to get involved in longer term projects that require depth and focus rather than immediate quick fixes, pursue work that allows you to develop your area of expertise, and structure your day and working environment to give you sizeable chunks of time where you can be absorbed in your work, in between smaller tasks and people-facing time.

● **your likely procrastination triggers:** unpredictability, erratic or emotional people, chaotic environments, conflict, feeling rushed or unprepared, lack of independence, public exposure

brilliant tip

Proactively agree expectations, outcomes and communication needs with colleagues to reduce the potential for interruptions and reactive working, negotiate time and space to work independently, practise stealth and camouflage, request meeting agendas upfront (explain this is how you can contribute your best ideas) and request time to think when a request puts you on the spot.

● **your biggest fears:** these are likely to be related around being wrong, especially if others criticise your work or spot a mistake, and taking risks when you don't have all the facts

brilliant tip

Watch out for your lizard brain when you feel threatened in these areas and be careful not to take mistakes too personally – sometimes things just don't work out and that's not always a bad thing, nor is it your fault.

- **what comes naturally to you:** in-depth research, complex problem solving, quality assurance, testing, probably anything that involves fine detail and facts

brilliant tip

What you're good at and enjoy, others may be actively procrastinating and resisting. Offer to help with the detail and not only will you be doing them a big favour, you'll also satisfy yourself that it's done properly.

- **what frustrates you:** mistakes, especially when they are a result of slipshod methods, lack of regard for rules or procedure, when people get 'carried away' by enthusiasm, when quality is sacrificed for speed or where your expertise has been overlooked or ignored.

brilliant tip

Expand your fact-finding to what motivates your colleagues (others may value speed, action or people above accuracy). Present your concerns as questions that provide insight to help them achieve their goal. Your eye for detail can be of service rather than criticism or road block to halt progress altogether.

What to tell your colleagues:

- 'Would you like me to give that a once over?'
- 'Shall I take a look into the detail for you?'
- 'What are the key factors of success here?'
- 'Can you send me the agenda on Monday so I can be prepared with my best ideas?'
- 'Let me think this through and come back to you with my questions/comments by Thursday.'
- 'Let me take this away and work on it. When do you need an update/the finished product by?'
- 'I'd like to get a full understanding of all the variables so I can crack on with putting the solution together. Rather than go back and forth with meetings and emails, can we book in a morning/afternoon to get it hammered out once and for all?'

 **action**

Read through each of these styles and identify your own DiSC style. Highlight the descriptions that resonate most with you, add your own thoughts and comments. Identify at least one motivator, procrastination trigger, fear, frustration and natural strength that relates to you and use the tips to make a personal action plan to tailor your personal productivity style.

Strengths and weaknesses

 'Everybody is a genius. But if you judge a fish by its ability to climb a tree, it will live its whole life believing that it is stupid.'

Albert Einstein

When talking about strengths and weaknesses, some people focus entirely on strengths and attempt to avoid or ignore their weaknesses. Other people focus on their weaknesses: the things they struggle with and stumble at, the thoughts of 'I'm too . . . ' or 'I'm not very . . . ', the areas they spend time, energy, money and attention trying to fix or improve.

Let's change the question: What's the hidden strength in your weakness?

Your strengths and weaknesses are not two separate things. They are two sides of the same coin. Every strength overused becomes a weakness, and every weakness hides a strength.

As Marianne Cantwell, author of *Be a Free Range Human,* put it: 'Our weaknesses are just our strengths in the wrong environment.'[1] It's where something we're really good at gets misused, overused, or simply used in a place where it isn't appreciated. Marianne's own love for change and seeking new solutions got her into trouble in her old job where she was being paid to follow the status quo, ask no questions and just get the job done, but now her fresh insights and incisive questions are exactly what her Free Range Humans love and value about her and pay her for.

---

brilliant **example**

I was bowled over recently by my nine-year-old's teacher at parents' evening. There are really only three things I want to know as a parent at parents' evening: How's my child doing? Is he in an environment where he can thrive? What can I do to help?

The teacher could have said: 'Yes, he's doing fine, well above what's expected. The only thing he needs to work on is his pace, as he can be a bit slow. This is what you can practise with him at home . . . '. But instead, he described our son as a thoughtful boy who cares about getting things right, a methodical ▶

learner who is hungry to learn and does best when he takes it step by step, a deep thinker you won't hear from for a while but when he does contribute to a group discussion he's worth listening to, and a powerful writer whose words are something his teacher looks forward to reading.

Now that's a teacher who knows my boy. And because of that, his classroom is an environment I know he'll thrive in. If he had only focused on the weakness, we would have known one tiny little fact about who he's not, and missed everything about who he is.

When you focus on your weakness, all you notice is who you are not. Where can you really go from there?

Overused strengths

Our weaknesses are not the opposite of our strengths. In fact they often stem from our strengths. They are strengths overused, for example:

- Drive can become stubbornness.
- Directness can become rude.
- Compassion can become people pleasing.
- An ability to make stuff happen can become control freakery.
- Attention to detail can become perfectionism.
- Thoughtful can become slow.
- Fast can become impatience.
- Improvisation can become unreliability.
- Imagination can become easily distracted.
- Possibility can become indecisiveness.

brilliant reflection

What happens when your strengths get overused?

Hidden strengths

What would you consider to be one of your weaknesses? Find the strength that's hidden within, and speak it out like it's a good thing.

For example, instead of 'I'm easily distracted by shiny new ideas' how about 'I have my best ideas at the most unexpected times, so I will make sure I'm always ready to capture them.'

Instead of 'I'm such a perfectionist' try 'I have high standards and take pride in my work. I may not be the fastest but I always deliver quality – I just need to remind myself to "deliver" that quality rather than perpetually edit and keep it to myself.'

When we identify the hidden strength within our weakness, we can start working with it, rather than fight it.

Harnessing strengths

What are your strengths? Where are your strengths most appreciated? What environment do you thrive best in? How often do you get to work in that environment? What changes could you make to your work or the way that you work, to operate from a place of strength more often?

What life-support or coping strategies do you need to put in place when you're not in that environment? As human beings we are very adaptable. While spending all your time out of your element is not advised, we can surprise ourselves with how much we can flex outside of our comfort zone when the purpose or situation calls.

↗ brilliant reflection

What can you do to nurture your strengths? What training could you pursue to develop your strengths? What opportunities would allow you to practice and grow your natural abilities? What support, mentoring or inspiration would feed that strength?

What do you need?

What do you need to give yourself? There are two parts to this question:

- What do you need?
- What do you give yourself?

Do you always give yourself what you need? How often do you give yourself a hard time, when what you really need is a break – or distraction when what you really need is focus? Do you give yourself more to worry about when what you need is clarity? Do you give yourself criticism when what you really need is encouragement?

✸ brilliant tip

What do you need to give yourself to be at your best? Because when you're at your best, you do your best work and you give your best to whoever you're with – at work, at home and everywhere else in life.

What do you need to give others?

It is often said, 'Treat other people how you would like to be treated', but what about how *they* would like to be treated? Different people have different needs.

 **brilliant** tip

Have an open conversation with the people you work with. Find out what they need to be motivated, to do their best thinking, to know that they are valued, or to deal with difficulties, conflict or setbacks? Ask them: 'What do you need?'

Embracing being human

Let's stop thinking we have to be perfect or entirely 'normal'. As human beings we sometimes defy logic. Everyone has their own foibles and quirks. That's what makes our contributions and creations more unique. Instead of hiding behind a mask of complete 'normality', what conversations can you have with those you live and work with?

- If you are easily distracted by shiny things, who could you give a heads up to, or permission to call out your magpie behaviour when it's not serving you well?

- If you find yourself getting bored or bogged down in detail, where would it be appropriate to openly admit that you may not have covered all the angles, who could you hand the baton over to, to cast an eagle eye over the finer details?

- If you have a tendency to be as subtle as a bull in a china shop, who would it be useful to forewarn that your directness doesn't necessarily mean you're upset, angry, dismissive or combative – you just tend to be economical with your words?

- If you don't think best on your feet, when might it be useful to say, 'Bear with me, I need some time to process this – let me come back to you'?

Being open about your personal style means that you can prepare and equip people with insights, tips and strategies on how they can best work with you. When they notice certain behaviours, they can have a better understanding about what that might mean (rather than assume what it would mean in their world) and what to do about it. It's not a blank pass to behave however you want, but rather a heads up to avoid offence and miscommunication and to promote better ways of working together, and permission to call you out, when you are not operating in your strengths – when you are underusing or overusing your strengths.

 **recap**

Understanding your personal style and preferences can help you to tap into your natural motivators, play to your strengths, and navigate your potential frustrations, fears and procrastination triggers, so that ultimately you can do more of your best work and enjoy what you do.

It can also help you to communicate better with the people you work with, and understand what you need individually and collectively to thrive and do your best work.

Ultimately when we give ourselves and each other permission to be fully human, we can stop wasting energy pretending, avoiding and fighting who we are, and start being brilliantly human.

References

[1] Cantwell, M., 2013. *Be a Free Range Human: Escape the 9–5, Create a Life You Love and Still Pay the Bills.* Kogan Page: London. www .beafreerangehuman.com

CHAPTER 8

Finding momentum and 'balance'

Are you working from home, or living at work? The truth is, there is life at work and life outside of work and being really productive depends on nurturing both.

This chapter provides the tools to help you develop a rhythm that is both consistent and flexible, that enables you to work with relentless focus and still switch off at the end of the day. It will challenge you to meet your basic human needs, show you how to do your best work fully charged rather than running on empty, and provide a fresh perspective on achievable, sustainable 'work–life balance'.

Daily rhythms

As human beings our energy levels vary throughout the day. We're not designed to be turned on and off with a constant output like a machine. We have peaks and troughs, times when we're fully switched on and raring to go, and times when we're more mellow, more easily distracted, or even completely zonked – and that's completely normal and natural. Instead of trying to change that, let's try and work with it.

Know your patterns

Are you an early bird or a night owl? Do you wake up with a zing, ready and raring to go? Or do you go slow in the morning, and come alive in the evening? When are you at your best? When's your prime time? What do you do with that time?

> ### ✸ brilliant tip
>
> Don't let your prime time get frittered away with emails, phone calls and other people's agendas. If you're a morning person, reserve the mornings to do your best work - the things that require your best attention. If you don't wake up fully until later in the day, use the morning to clear the clutter that doesn't require your best energy – point and click, form filling, filing, quick wins and bitty jobs - so that when you're fully on form in the afternoon, you can focus your best energy on the things that really matter.

Manage attention, not time

In *How to be a Productivity Ninja,* Graham Allcott suggests thinking about your attention levels in three categories:

1 Proactive attention (when you're on full form).

2 Active attention (awake, reasonably alert).

3 Inactive attention (brain dead, zombie mode, physically here but no one's home).

Your attention levels will vary during the day – being aware of them means you can decide what's best to tackle in each mode, as Graham puts it: 'You'll start to realise that it's a criminal waste to be changing the printer cartridge during a period of proactive attention. It's like using a sledgehammer to crack a nut, although in that moment it probably feels no different to when you change the printer cartridge at any other time.'[1]

Know your landscape

Your energy and attention levels don't just depend on the time of day. They also vary according to what else is going on around that time. Have you had a day full of meetings or a heavy week of travelling? Are you battling the flu or do you have a child that's battling sleep? That's likely to affect your energy and attention levels.

What else have you got in your diary or on your to-do list? Are they tasks and activities that energise you or drain you? If my husband has a people-intensive week, the chances are he'll be pretty exhausted. If I've spent a morning staring at spreadsheets, I will have very little attention left for screen-work, whereas I'd positively welcome a coaching conversation or a networking meeting.

🔼 brilliant reflection

Do the candle test. What energises you? What drains you? Use this exercise to help scope your landscape and manage your energy:

1   Draw a candle.
2   Next to the flame, make a list of tasks, activities and environments that energise you. What makes you come alive? What do you enjoy doing so much that it gives you energy? Write those things down next to the flame.
3   Next to the wax, make a note of tasks and activities that drain you. What takes energy out of you? What leaves you drained? They could be things you are perfectly competent and perhaps even very good at doing, but ultimately if you do too much of it, you end up running on empty.

Now use this to gauge your day or week ahead. How much of your time and energy are you spending 'in the flame'? How much are you spending 'in the wax'? How does this affect your energy levels?

To improve your energy and create a more sustainable rhythm, consider:

● How could you spend more time 'in the flame' and less time 'in the wax'? ▶

- Is the wax supporting your flame or drowning it?
- What flame activity could you introduce to brighten up a 'waxy' day?
- How could you mix and match your 'flame' and 'wax' activities to regulate your energy levels during the day?
- What could you move from the 'wax' into the 'flame' by changing the way you work? (e.g. if business planning drains you but being outdoors gives you energy, could you take your planning session outdoors and combine it with a walk?)

Starting the day well

How do you start the day? Do you stumble out of bed and go through the motions like a zombie? Do you race around tending to a million and one things clambering for your attention from the moment your alarm goes off? Do you slide the alarm off on your phone and go straight into your emails?

How do you wake up?

Some people swear by their early morning workouts – it gets their blood pumping and their brains and bodies working first thing in the morning. I have to admit, the days when I do manage to go for a 7 am run, I feel great! Other people prefer a much gentler start – perhaps with a gentle stretch, or some peaceful meditation. A quiet cup of tea with their brains to themselves – perhaps in one of those cups that say 'Shh . . . don't talk to me yet'.

brilliant example

One of my friends finds that sitting up in bed, doing some gentle stretches and drinking a glass of water before getting up helps her to wake up properly before going into 'do' mode. Another friend finds that getting out of bed as soon as the alarm goes off, instead of staying in bed for 'just a few minutes more', helps to snap her out of her morning lethargy. My colleague Katy recently discovered that 'power posing' in bed for five to ten minutes before she gets up in the morning makes her feel a lot happier, more energised and less groggy.[2]

Getting into work mode

Our brains are wired up to notice patterns and signals. What signals trigger your brain to switch between home mode and work mode? If you travel to an office, the commute might be when that transition happens. If you work from home however, you might need to create or recreate that signal.

brilliant example

A financial advisor I know was relishing the prospect of ditching his suit when he started working from home, only to find that it was only when he put his tie on, that he felt 'at work'. Another friend created his own commute by walking round the block each morning and evening to start and finish his work day. My husband even found that when he started working from home, drinking from a designated 'work cup' helped to put him in work mode!

Of course, there's nothing wrong with working from home in your pyjamas, as long as you find your own way of getting into work mode (and no one else can see you). Think about the little things you could do, to give yourself those signals that it's time to get to work, from simple things like having breakfast or having a shave to putting on a piece of music, listening to your regular morning radio show or meditating for ten minutes.

Check in with yourself first

It's tempting to check your emails first thing in the morning. Especially if you have your smartphone doubling up as an alarm on charge next to your bed. But when you check in with the rest of the world before checking in with yourself, it's very easy to let someone else's agenda dictate your day. One piece of bad news can set the mood and tone of your day. One unforeseen problem or opportunity can take you on a tangent before you've had a chance to decide what's really important from your perspective.

The world is full of messages. It's amazing how easy it is to be buffeted from one thing to another when you're not clear on your own agenda, and spend the day reacting to whoever or whatever's shouting the loudest. It makes a big difference to have half an hour in the morning to check in with yourself first, before you check in with the rest of the world.

For example:

- Writing your 'hit list' for the day – your top 1–3 must do's – on a Post-it note before turning on your email.

- Setting your Outlook to open up to Calendar or Task View as a default, rather than the Inbox.

- If you're a Google Chrome user, check out the 'Momentum' extension where you can set your focus for the day and be inspired and reminded of it every time you open a new browser tab.

Choose your focus

 **example**

The other day, I didn't want to get up. It was grey and wet outside, and I was warm and sleepy in my bed. I was tired when I got up, when I got the kids ready, when I questioned why yet again we were trying to find stuff when it was time to go, when I marched my daughter straight into a puddle outside her classroom, because I didn't notice it, because I was tired.

I realised I needed to choose something. Otherwise tiredness would choose me. I chose to wake up. I chose to go for a run in the pouring rain, which was strangely refreshing, once I abandoned the notion of staying dry! I made my neighbour smile, and the road-workers too, which made me smile (always happy to be of service). It worked: I woke up. I was still tired, but I was awake, and alive – and that made a big difference to me and my day.

What about you? If you don't fancy a run in the rain, never in a million years, that's alright. It's your choice, and that's the point.

If you've got a clear day in front of you, what are you choosing to fill it with? If you have a busy day ahead, packed full of commitments, how are you choosing to approach it – with panic or enthusiasm, dread or determination? That difficult conversation you need to have: what will you choose – patience, compassion, assertiveness or even bullishness?

The stressful environment at work, where everyone's feeling the pressure and sniping at each other – will you choose to join in, or buck the trend and be the one who smiles contagiously? That thing that takes you outside your comfort zone – will you choose avoidance, reluctance or will you choose to throw yourself in fully? The situation beyond your control, the one that's painful, difficult and unavoidable – will you choose to live in frustration and disappointment, or in courage, hope, faith, kindness, humour or the company of good friends around you?

brilliant tip

Whatever's going on, you always have a choice. Sometimes it's a big choice, sometimes it's a little one. Sometimes it will transform the world around you. Other times it will just transform you. What are YOU choosing for today?

Maintaining momentum (or what to do when the work never ends)

Does this ring a bell? 'Every day I start with a bulging to-do list, full of energy and optimism to charge ahead. Come on, bring it on, let's do this thing. By lunchtime my energy starts waning and the end is nowhere near in sight. By the end of the day, I'm knackered, disappointed, bewildered (where did the time go?) and proceed to shuffle what's left to an already full list for tomorrow.'

Whether you're working on a long-term project, tackling a relentless workload, or just find that there's always more to do, it can be hard to find momentum and motivation, and easy for inertia and procrastination to set in. After all, if there's just more work ahead, what's the incentive for getting on with it and getting it done? But if you're constantly working and never stop, you can find yourself losing interest, passion and joy. The work you love becomes drudgery, and you burn out.

When the work never ends, it's up to you to create your own finish line, to define for yourself what 'job done' looks like.

Without a finish line, it's easy to lose momentum, and for the project to creep. The product is never quite ready to be launched, the presentation still needs tweaking, the campaign becomes so long and arduous, you find yourself reluctantly trudging along rather than powering through.

Without a finish line, it's easy to get distracted by shiny things ('I'll just take a look at this first') or quick wins ('I'll just deal with this first . . . oh and that one . . .'). And get stalled by the enormity of it all ('Woah! That's a long way to go, I'm going to have to wait until I have more time. Better make that cup of tea . . .').

When there's a finish line in sight, you've got something to aim for. It gives you direction, definition and a reason to muster up the strength and sprint ahead.

brilliant example

Freya was someone who had a tendency to go all guns blazing at the beginning of a project, full of enthusiasm and adrenaline, so much so that in those early days, it would not be unusual for her to get more done than she set out to do. She'd power through her to-do list, find she still had time left in the day, and add a few more jobs in. But after a while she'd burn out. She'd run out of energy. And start becoming aware of everything else in life she had put on hold, then wonder how on earth she could ever fit it all in.

Instead of going as fast as she could for as long as she could, she decided to pace herself, and honour a daily finish line when she would be 'done   ▶

for the day'. Whenever she got to the end of her to-do list, she gave herself permission to stop, instead of doing 'just one more thing'.

The result? She found herself with far more energy. Instead of running as fast as she could for the first couple of days, and running out of steam, she was able to keep pace, and keep going. Yes, there were peaks and troughs – some weeks were more productive than others, but ultimately she procrastinated less, got more done, took more breaks and enjoyed greater satisfaction. She got everything she wanted to get done in time, and proved to herself that she could do it without killing herself.

The bad news is, the work never ends. But the good news is we get to create our own finish lines. We get to define what job done looks like. When we honour those finish lines, when we enjoy life beyond the finish line, each race is satisfying, and we find we have more than enough to keep going.

 reflection

Where's your finish line each day? When are you done for the day?

Switching off, fuelling up

 'Almost everything will work again if you unplug it for a few minutes, including you.'

Anne Lamott

Sometimes our brains need actively distracting from work. It can be easy to physically leave the office, close down our laptops, and still be at work in our heads. We often associate productivity with work: a productive day is usually a day when we've set goals, gotten stuff done, worked hard, and achieved what we set out to do. But how do you spend your downtime?

Is it more of an afterthought – something you'll figure out once you get there, if you get there? Is it something you put off, telling yourself, 'I'll take time off when I've got everything done'? Do you cram it full of chores and odd jobs: 'Day off: laundry, fix door, get hair cut, buy Christmas presents, pay electricity bill, sort out filing pile, wash car . . .'?

We often see our downtime as unproductive and to an extent unimportant. We downplay it, delay it, avoid it and when we do find ourselves with it, we don't know what to do with it. We've forgotten how to deal with downtime, let alone how to value it, so much so that we're more likely to feel guilty, struggle to justify or even apologise for having some downtime.

Which is completely and utterly ridiculous.

To recharge is to restore your capacity. Without charge there is no productivity. Recharging is productive. Recharging is not a luxury. It is fuel for our productivity.

The wobbly line

Nobody understands this more than athletes. When an athlete finishes a match, a game or a race, the last thing they will do is go straight back in the gym, or start another match or do more training. It would be completely unthinkable. Athletes understand something that often the rest of us overlook: that recovery is a crucial part of our job. What we do when we're not performing directly impacts how well we perform. Our tendency to work under pressure without any breaks is completely counterproductive.

Psychologist and workplace resilience specialist Rob Archer asks, 'How wobbly is your line? As human beings we are designed to have periods of high performance followed by periods of recovery, activity followed by rest, and breaks in between the work. Our natural rhythm follows a 'wobbly line' that goes up and down. That's how we sustain peak performance and health.'[3]

brilliant reflection

How wobbly is your line? Does it go up and down? Or does it just flat line (which is never a good sign with anything living!)?

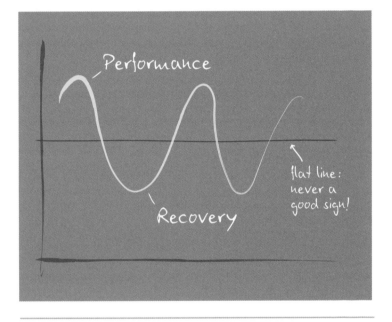

To work and live well we need to have a rhythm of recovery – daily, weekly, monthly, seasonally – even yearly. Time away from the work to recharge so we come back fully fuelled rather than running on empty.

Standby

How do you spend your downtime? Do you actually recharge – or do you just go on standby, waiting to get back to work again? Get home, down tools, veg out, sit in front of the telly, surf the net, play some inane game – anything that doesn't require brain-power, but keeps your brain occupied enough that it doesn't completely shut down or start firing up again.

It's an easy option, and doesn't require much thought or setting up. You can do it pretty much anywhere, especially if you have Candy Crush on your phone. And it does conserve energy to a degree, but only gives minimal recharge, if any at all.

There are certain things I know I default to, that put me on standby rather than actually recharge me. I know because I get pulled towards them for that instant light relief, but a couple of hours later, I feel just as drained as I did before – except it's now later and I'm a couple of hours closer to when I need to be back on form.

Solitude vs company

If you've had an intensive week of meetings, conferences and being with people, you may find that you crave solitude, some 'cave time' to recharge. If you've been chained to your desk all week, writing proposals and fiddling with spreadsheets you might find yourself craving some company and good conversation.

This is particularly the case if you are an introvert who has an intensive people-facing job, or an extrovert who spends a lot of time in solitude. Generally speaking, introverts recharge in solitude whereas extroverts are energised by the company of other people. Many introvert leaders schedule in solitude – a weekend every six weeks or a 24-hour period once a month for example, where they block out in the diary in advance and commit to as an essential part of their rhythm. On the other hand, if you're an extrovert who spends a lot of time chained to your desk in front of a screen, you may find that a night out with friends can give you more energy than an evening sat in front of the TV.

Retreat

In a battle, when someone shouts 'Retreat!' you get the sense that things aren't going so well. It's a last resort, a failure, a sign of weakness. But if you think of a spa retreat – that signifies indulgence, something to relish, enjoy and welcome. It's an opportunity to rest from the day to day and time to indulge and nurture.

What would be a retreat for you – something that indulges you and feeds your soul? For some it might be a long soak in a bubble bath with a good book. For others, it might involve getting your hands dirty in a garage with a whole load of tools, engines and oil. Some people find pottering in the garden or baking a perfect retreat. Others would much rather run through mud or swim in a freezing cold lake!

Recreation

Recharging isn't always about rest (although it doesn't happen without some kind of rest). Sometimes it's about doing something active. Going for a run, spending time with friends, laughing, being outdoors, singing, reading, cooking, dancing or going down a zip-wire with your kids – are all things that require you to do something – but can be recharging all the same.

What do you enjoy doing so much that it leaves you feeling more alive and recharged than before? What activities, company and environments actively energise you?

Fuel

What fires you up? What charges your creativity and motivation? What fuels your inspiration? Twenty minutes watching a TED talk, a geek-out conversation over lunch, or taking a day to attend a conference and network with inspiring people reminds me why I'm doing what I'm doing and does wonders for my motivation and productivity. What is fuel for you? Where do you go for it? How often do you tap into it?

Twenty tiny moments of joy

Rob Archer notes, 'Everybody gets tired, but exhaustion is different. Classically our reaction to being exhausted is to cut back on the things that give us meaning, purpose and joy. We disengage to conserve our energy, but when we do that, we squeeze out the joy in life and all that remains is the treadmill – and when you combine exhaustion with lack of joy, that's fertile ground for burnout and ill health.'[4]

One useful exercise to combat exhaustion is to compile a list of twenty tiny things that bring you joy. Not big things like, 'When I'm on top of Mount Kilimanjaro' or 'When I got married' but tiny things like smelling freshly cut flowers or the way your dog screws up his face when you scratch his head. Tiny things you can do, have or experience in the day to day that bring you joy.

 **action**

Start your list now - what would some of your twenty tiny things be?

1 _____

2 _____

3 _____

4 _____

5 _____

6 _____

7 _____ ▶

8 _____

9 _____

10 _____

11 _____

12 _____

13 _____

14 _____

15 _____

16 _____

17 _____

18 _____

19 _____

20 _____

Basic human needs

Let's go back to basics for a minute. In 1943 Abraham Maslow proposed in his paper 'A Theory of Human Motivation' that there are five hierarchical levels of human needs:

1 **Physiological needs:** air, food, drink, shelter, warmth, sex, sleep.

2 **Safety needs:** protection from elements, security, order, law, stability, freedom from fear.

3 **Love and belongingness needs:** friendship, intimacy, affection and love from work, family, friends, romantic relationships.

4 **Esteem needs:** achievement, mastery, independence, status, dominance, prestige, self-respect, respect from others.

5 **Self-actualisation needs:** realising personal potential, self-fulfilment, seeking personal growth and peak experiences.

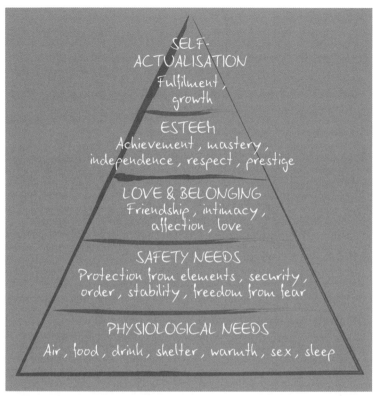

Source: Maslow, A.H., 1943. 'A theory of human motivation', *Psychological Review* 50(4): 370–396. This content is in the public domain.

So why is it that we think we can sacrifice sleep as long as we have enough self-fulfilment or that prestige will compensate for a lack of close relationships?

It's true that the higher needs are our true motivators – the more we get, the more it fuels our motivation. Whereas the lower levels are what Maslow referred to as 'deficiency needs' – they are strong drivers when they are unmet, but once they are met, they no longer fuel us. Once we have enough food or sleep, getting more generally doesn't really excite us! But we do need to meet them, our basic human needs.

Here are the three things people most often neglect when they are 'too busy'.

Sleep

We all know we need it. But it's often one of the first things to go when faced with a crazy schedule, overwhelming workload or impending deadline. In fact, with comments like 'I can sleep when I'm dead' and 'The most successful CEOs only have four hours' sleep' it's almost become a competition to see who can get away with the least amount of sleep.

Research increasingly suggests that 'the short-term productivity gains from skipping sleep to work are quickly washed away by the detrimental effects of sleep deprivation on your mood, ability to focus, and access to higher-level brain functions for days to come. The negative effects of sleep deprivation are so great that people who are drunk outperform those lacking sleep.'[5]

Lack of sleep affects our high-level brain function: our ability to think logically, process information, pay attention, and think creatively – all the things we need to do our work well. It affects our mood, resilience and relationships – making us more easily irritated or upset, less objective, more likely to take things personally, more prone to misunderstanding and more reactive to stress. It affects our health: from colds that take weeks to shake, headaches, coughs, infections, loss of voice (a highly inconvenient occupational hazard for teachers and trainers) existing conditions that get triggered (my husband's bad back gets aggravated by lack of sleep) to more serious health conditions – cancer, heart disease, type-2 diabetes, infections and obesity have all been linked to reduced sleep.[6]

It also affects our memory and routines: forgetting to put the milk in the porridge, losing keys in the fridge, forgetting to lock the door, missing the turning that we take every single day to work – things we take for granted and usually do without thinking, we forget to do when we're tired. We become more prone to making mistakes, and we can do more damage than good. Bill Clinton, who's made some pretty famous mistakes, said on CNN in 2008: 'Most of the mistakes I made, I made when I was too tired, because I tried too hard and worked too hard. You make better decisions when you're not too tired.[7]

Diet and hydration

Convenience food, skipping meals, surviving on a diet of chocolate and coffee – are all common tactics to resort to when pressed for time, but this too can be a quick fix that ends up costing you more.

Going hungry doesn't help. If you put 'hunger' as one of your culprits for distraction in Chapter 2, you'll be pleased to know that you have scientific backing. Your brain needs fuel to function, and that fuel is glucose – 25 grams of glucose in fact 'about the amount found in a banana', according to brain researcher Leigh Gibson.[8]

How you get that glucose doesn't affect brain function immediately, but quick release sugars will cause spikes and slumps in glucose levels that mess with our ability to concentrate – which explains why it's so hard to stay awake in meetings that occur straight after a carb-heavy lunch, and why eating sugary foods makes you crave more. Whereas slow release foods, like oats, or combining sugar with protein will give a more steady level of focus and attention.

'Adequate nutrition can raise your productivity levels by 20 per cent on average' according to the World Health Organization, who recommend dark chocolate, nuts, seeds as great foods to snack on for productivity.

Dehydration also affects our productivity. The human brain is made up of 75 per cent water and even mild dehydration can affect our mental performance as well as our mood and physical energy. It's often been said that once you're thirsty, it's already too late. If you're feeling sluggish or foggy, chances are you may well be dehydrated.

Exercise

Exercising releases endorphins, makes us happier and keeps our bodies active and healthy – and it also gets our brains working better. Brain activity increases after a 20-minute walk, compared to sitting still, and a study by the University of Bristol found that 'On exercise days, people's mood significantly improved after exercising. Mood stayed about the same on days they didn't, with the exception of people's sense of calm which deteriorated.'[9]

Many clients and workshop delegates I've worked with have reported that doing some exercise before work or during the working day has helped them to be more charged, focused and creative in their work. Taking a walk or even just standing up can change our brain activity and get us thinking differently. The same goes for walking meetings and stand-up meetings. Changing our physiology changes our thinking. Our brains have evolved to solve problems on the move: 'exercise physically remodels our brains for peak performance . . . and is essential for helping the brain and body recover from stress, learning and cognitive renewal' says Professor John Ratey.[10]

Safety, love and belonging

It's also worth remembering that safety, love and belonging needs are also essential needs in the pyramid. Our sense of security and certainty and the health and quality of our relationships at work also affect our productivity. Working in a hostile or toxic environment can be a real productivity killer – however personally motivated or brilliantly organised you are. Operating in a season of a high level of unpredictability and insecurity will take its toll in energy and attention. Major life changes from getting married, having children and moving house to divorce, bereavement and family issues all have an impact on how we show up at work.

Pretending these things don't affect us can consume valuable attention and energy that's already in short supply. Giving ourselves and our colleagues permission to show up as human is far more effective for our wellbeing and our productivity, and when we have the opportunity to support each other as fellow human beings, we create strong working relationships and genuine friendships that transform both the quality of our work as well as the quality of our life at work.

One-point improvements

We all know this to a degree, but how do we get back on track? It's one thing to know that looking after our physical needs will improve our productivity, but how do we change our habits when life is busy and shortcutting on our basic needs has become an accepted way of life? Here are some ways to get started with small steps:

- Create a relaxing bedtime routine.
- Aim for one early night a week.
- Try a screen-free evening.
- Bulk cook meals and freeze in portions.
- Stock fruit, nuts and dark chocolate as snacks.
- Have a glass of water next to your bed, and drink it before you get up in the morning.
- Keep a drink of water on your desk (a friend of mine even used her 'coffee to go' cup for this).
- Take phone calls standing up.
- Get a stand-up desk or an adjustable one.
- Have walking or stand-up meetings.
- Take a walk at lunch times.
- Do desk stretches.
- Keep a stock of healthy breakfast supplies at work.

- Encourage healthy eating at work with an office weekly shop where healthy snacks come out of the office budget, and unhealthy snacks are paid for by the individuals themselves.

- Have a shower at the office for those who want to cycle to work or go for a lunchtime run.

Beyond the 9-5

Does the 9–5 job still exist? For most people it's becoming a myth. From teachers who work up to nearly 60 hours a week[11] to senior directors who regularly spend 30–40 hours just in meetings, then try and catch up on emails and the 'real work' at home. Even for those whose hours are less extreme, many people admit to staying a little later, arriving a little earlier, and taking work home to 'catch up'.

Longer hours don't work

The law of diminishing returns states that not every extra hour put in will generate the same output. Henry Ford's experiments on productivity found that 40 hours per week was the optimum number of hours for his production line employees. When they worked past those forty hours, their productivity would diminish.

For work that requires intense focus, this number is even less. Most creators and writers find that they only have a couple of hours of proactive attention, when they are at their best, coming up with their best ideas, doing their best work. After that, they can work on other stuff – but their attention levels are nowhere near the same.

We all have our optimum level of working. Beyond that, each extra hour we put in will cost more and give us less in return.

Working from home or living at work?

With the increase of flexible working and 24/7 technology, the lines that used to define work have become blurred. Which gives us a challenge and an opportunity.

The opportunity is, it gives us flexibility. With increasing flexibility we get to define our own hours. We can choose to get to the office earlier to avoid the rush hour traffic or later to fit in the school run. We can take ourselves for a run at lunchtime because it clears our mind and forms part of our marathon training. We can fit in that meeting for the social enterprise we're setting up while we're in London for work. We can negotiate flexible working from home to fit around care commitments, or work on the beach whilst travelling. We can pursue part-time study, or set up our own business without quitting the job that pays the bills.

The challenge is when everything's possible and there are no set rules to fall back on, it's up to us to define our hours. We need to choose our hours rather than end up working all hours. It's easy to do that one extra hour, send that one last email, say yes to that one extra commitment, check that one last time when it's already way past your bedtime. It's hard to say 'I'm not at work right now' when your work follows you wherever you go. And when others are practising flexibility, we can find ourselves adopting their hours as well as our own – if your boss is emailing you at 7 am on Saturday morning, does that mean you should be replying then too?

'Balance'

Most people say they want a better work–life balance. They want to be productive at work so that they can go home on time, 'switch off', and have a life outside of work. But in reality 'work–life balance' has become a holy grail that no one seems to get.

It's supposed to get us working less and enjoying life more, but in reality, it has us striving for perfection and counting the hours we spend at work, the hours we spend with our family, at the gym, even in bed, trying to get the elusive 'right' combination.

It's created a superhero syndrome, where it's no longer good enough to just be good at one thing. We have to be great at everything, flying high at work, going the extra mile and exceeding expectations, raising great kids, taking every opportunity to provide the best we can for them – from what we feed them, where we take them on holiday to how much extra reading we do with them, keeping ourselves fit and healthy, our relationships alive and well, giving back with our voluntary and community involvements, all the while having an immaculate home. We have to be all things to all people, and it's exhausting just thinking about it!

It's also become a source of guilt. We're constantly counting the hours that go by and worrying that we're not spending enough time elsewhere.

The problem with work–life balance is we've turned something that was intended to give us a break into something we beat ourselves up with. Perhaps it's time to let go of work–life balance. It was a man-made invention after all.

Here are some alternative propositions instead:

Work–life rhythm

Having a work–life rhythm means there are highs and lows and ebbs and flow to your life, instead of trying to make everything uniform and 'balanced'. There are times when you need to run fast and times when you need to slow down and be still.

Instead of trying to slow down the fast times and speed up the slow, let's run with life when it speeds up. Let's treat rest and renewal as essential to our productivity. Let's embrace the wild rides, soak up the quiet lulls and enjoy everything in between.

Work–life integrity

Are you the same person at work and outside of work? Yes, you may adapt your behaviour to suit the situation, but deep down, are you being the same person, with the same values, identity and purpose?

Work–life integrity is not so much to do with the hours you spend, but who you are being at work. When you are true to yourself at work, there is a sense of peace that comes with it. When there's a conflict with your core values, no matter how much you achieve, work will lack meaning and satisfaction, and life will feel out of balance.

The same applies to life outside of work. Sometimes, when you are doing work that you love, the challenge is to be the same fired up, passionate person at home, with grumpy teenagers and tired toddlers, when you might be equally tired and grumpy yourself. One CEO admitted recently, 'People at work thank us more, they appreciate our contributions, they think we're brilliant. I can't always say the same for my family!'

Work–life integrity is about being equally mindful of who we are being both at work and outside of work, so that the way we live and work honours the values that matter most to us.

Work-life quality

We all have crazy seasons, when one part of our life takes over the others, but just because we don't have as much time for the other parts of our life, it doesn't mean we can't enjoy them as much.

The quality of your life at work matters too. Hours are not the only way to measure how consuming work can be. Conflict, difficult relationships, lack of appreciation, lack of connection or community, uncertainty, stress and being constantly over-whelmed can all contribute to a low quality of life at work, that takes far more out of you than time spent in a positive, productive environment.

Instead of obsessing over hours, let's make sure the quality of life at work and life outside of work is good. Because when our life at work is good, we are naturally more productive and happier at home. When our life at home is good, the quality of our work improves. Our wellbeing and productivity are inextricably linked, both in and outside of work.

 **recap**

True productivity is not about trying to run harder and faster on the hamster wheel for as long as possible. We do our best work when know how to start and how to stop, how to create momentum and how to switch off. When we take recharging seriously and give ourselves what we need to be at our best, we naturally do our best work. That's when life is good - both at work and outside of work - and that's when the two work well together.

References

[1] Allcott, G., 2014. *How to be a Productivity Ninja: Worry Less, Achieve More and Love What You Do.* Icon Books: London.

[2] Bateson, K. 'Ready, steady, power pose!', *Productive Magazine!* Available at: http://productivemag.com/28/ready-steady-power-pose#

[3] Dr Rob Archer, The Career Psychologist. Available at: www.thecareer psychologist.com

[4] Ibid.

[5] Bradberry, T., 2015. 'Sleep deprivation is killing you and your career', research from Division of Sleep Medicine at the Harvard Medical School. Available at: www.inc.com/travis-bradberry/sleep-deprivation-is-killing-you-and-your-career.html

[6] Gallagher, J., 2014. '"Arrogance" of ignoring need for sleep', BBC News. Available at: www.bbc.co.uk/news/health-27286872

[7] Rock, L. and McVeigh, T. (eds) 'It's time to stop this competitive sleep deprivation', *The Guardian*. Available at: www.theguardian.com/theobserver/she-said/2014/may/16/its-time-to-stop-this-competitive-sleep-deprivation

[8] Widrich, L., 2012. 'How your productivity is determined by what you eat', Buffer. Available at: https://blog.bufferapp.com/the-science-behind-how-your-nutrition-will-decide-your-productivity-for-today

[9] Press release. http://www.bristol.ac.uk/news/2008/6063.html

[10] John Ratey, M.D. Available at: www.johnratey.com

[11] Arnett, G., 2013. 'Who works the most hours – MPs or teachers?', *The Guardian*. Available at: www.theguardian.com/news/datablog/2013/apr/23/who-works-most-teachers-or-mps

CHAPTER 9

Overcoming 'overwhelm'

S tress, guilt and the feeling of being overwhelmed are often the symptoms that drive you to improve your productivity, but a life driven by stress, overwhelm and guilt is not a brilliant, or productive, one. This chapter will show you how these factors affect your productivity, and provides guidance on how to change the way you respond to them to take back control and work more productively and effectively.

Navigating overwhelm

Ever have the feeling that you're chasing your own thoughts around your head? Try and pinpoint a thought and it seems to run away and spiral into several other thoughts. Try to work out a problem and the more you think about it the worse it seems to get. Try and focus on one thing you need to move forward on and several other jobs start nagging at you.

Here are three simple steps to help you regain a sense of clarity and control when you find yourself feeling overwhelmed with 'everything':

Empty your head

David Allen, author of *Getting Things Done* says: 'Your mind is for having ideas, not for holding them.'[1] The more you try and keep in your head, the less headspace you have to think with.

It's really hard to gain perspective when everything is in your head and you can't see the wood for the trees. When everything is close up, in your face, demanding your attention. It's also harder to separate your thoughts and your feelings, your reality from your fear, evidence from imagination: fear and difficulty can often appear larger in your head.

What's on your mind? The first step to overcoming overwhelm is to get it out of your head and capture onto paper (or a screen) where you can see it all in one place and start to make sense of it.

 **action**

Go grab a pen and paper – or better still, a stack of Post-it notes – and ask yourself, 'What's on my mind?'. Then write. Write everything down – things you need to do, things you're concerned about, things you're trying to remember, projects you have on the go, errands you need to run, people you need to call, ideas you have knocking around your head. Simply do a brain dump and empty your head.

Work vs worry

Not everything you worry about is within your control. Not everything you write down will have something you can do about it. Sometimes the greatest source of overwhelm comes from feeling obligated without being in control. Having a responsibility over a situation without the capability or capacity to do something about it. This is when you need to separate the worry from the work.

 **action**

A useful exercise to do this is Stephen Covey's Circles of Concern and Influence, taken from *The 7 Habits of Highly Effective People*.[2] On a large sheet of paper, draw two circles – one inside the other. For each item you have written down, ask yourself: 'Can I do something about this?'

If the answer is no, put it in the outer circle. Covey calls this the Circle of Concern. These are the things that may impact you but you have no control over.

If the answer is yes, put it in the inner circle. This is your Circle of Influence. These are the things you can do something about.

Take a look at the overall picture. How much of your focus is in your Circle of Concern? How much of your time and attention is taken up by worry over things that are beyond your control?

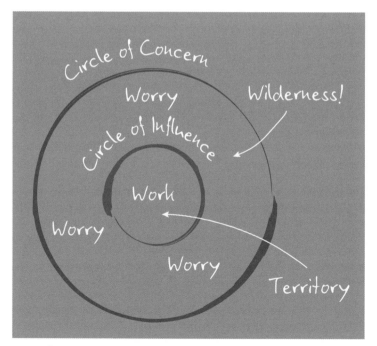

Source: After Covey, S.R., 2005. *The 7 Habits of Highly Effective People.* Simon & Schuster: London. Reproduced with permission.

Choose your focus: you can choose to spend your time and energy worrying about all the things beyond your control (and there will be plenty to keep you busy there), or you can focus on the work that is within your control. Your choice.

Clarify actions

There is a difference between brain dumps and to-do lists. The purpose of a brain dump is to clear your head. It can be a collection of big projects and small tasks, ideas, reminders and commitments. The purpose of a to-do list is to enable action. When you treat your brain dump as a to-do list, there is too much choice, too much to do, and no sense of clarity and definition. It can be overwhelming, trying to decide what to do first.

 **action**

Take a look at your inner circle – your Circle of Influence. For each thing you've written down, ask yourself: 'Am I clear what I need to do here?'

If you've written something like 'Sort website' or 'Charlie's behaviour', it might be within your sphere of influence, but if you haven't identified what you need to do about it, then it will remain a worry rather than something you can actually work on.

To identify the work, ask yourself: 'What do I need to do about this?' There might be several things that come to mind. Make a note of them. If you're using Post-it notes, put each thing on a separate note. Then ask yourself: 'What's the first thing I need to do about this?'. Then make sure that one is at the top of the pile and the one you can see when you look at your Circle of Influence.

Repeat this until everything in your Circle of Influence is a clear action that you can take. Now you have your work.

How does stress affect your productivity?

Stress has become commonplace in working life (and arguably every other part of life too). You can experience stress when there's too much work, when there's not enough work, when everything happens at once, and when nothing seems to be happening. You can get stressed about the demands other people have of you – and the expectations you place on yourself. You can experience stress over a wide range of situations, from the state of the economy or the environment, to finding socks, parking spaces and grey hairs. 'I'm stressed' has become part of everyday vocabulary even in school children.

What actually happens when you get stressed? And is it always a bad thing?

Psychologist Rob Archer suggests that 'human beings are well evolved to deal with acute stress, but less well evolved to deal with chronic stress'.[3]

Acute stress happens when something puts immediate pressure on you to act. Like being chased by a lion. The human stress response primes your body to move quickly to stay alive: your attention span narrows, giving you extreme focus on one thing. Energy is diverted away from less immediately essential systems, such as your immune or digestive systems, to your big muscles (so that you can run and stay alive!).

Of course, in modern life your stresses are likely to be psychological rather than facing actual lions. As a human being, you have the capacity to create stress in any situation: when you have a difficult conversation, a big decision to make, changes to navigate or deadlines to meet, for example. When it comes to productivity, the acute stress response can actually be quite useful: when you're firefighting an emergency or working to a tight deadline, energy to move and increased focus is not a bad thing to have at all.

The problem comes when acute stress becomes chronic stress. When there are five different emergencies all crying out for your attention, you become overwhelmed and lose your focus. When your energy becomes depleted because you're constantly in emergency mode, you become exhausted. When your digestive and immune systems have been shut down for too long, your health suffers. As a human being you're probably never going to be caught by a lion, but you can be caught by fatigue.

The answer isn't to avoid stress. As Rob Archer explains: 'If I care about something, I will stress about it. To avoid a life of stress would be to avoid a life of meaning. What we need to do is make sure that the stress we experience is in service of the things we care about – and that we are strategic about how we spend and recover our energy.'

Stanford University psychologist Kelly McGonigal also suggests that how you think about your stress also changes its impact on your health. One study found that people who experienced a lot of stress – and believed that stress is harmful for your health – had a 43 per cent increased risk of dying. But people who experienced a lot of stress but did not view stress as harmful actually had the lowest risk of dying of anyone in the study, including people who had relatively little stress.

In her TED talk, 'How to make stress your friend', Kelly McGonigal explains that 'when you change your mind about stress, you can change your body's response to stress'.[4] Instead of seeing stress as harmful, she suggests seeing the stress response as a sign that your body is energised and preparing you to meet a challenge – like an athlete about to start a race.

One of the acute responses to stress is that heart rate goes up and breathing increases, to deliver more oxygen to the brain. In a typical stress response, blood vessels constrict when heart rate goes up, which is one of the reasons that chronic stress is sometimes associated with cardiovascular disease. However,

McGonigal found that when participants viewed their stress response as helpful for their performance, they were less anxious and more confident, their heart was still pounding but their blood vessels stayed relaxed. 'It actually looks a lot like what happens in moments of joy and courage.'

brilliant tip

Choose to see stress differently. Use the energy it creates to help you prepare for the challenge ahead.

Is guilt stealing your time?

In the quest for productivity there is a lot of focus on time, organisation, tools, schedules, techniques, emails, distraction, interruptions, motivation, mindset, vision, action, procrastination, deadlines and focus.

But there's something else that everyone recognises, but no one explicitly talks about. That thing is guilt.

- 'I feel guilty when I'm working and not there for my kids . . . and when I'm with my kids and not working.'
- 'I feel guilty that I'm neglecting my health, but also when I take time off for me.'
- 'I feel guilty when I have to work late . . . and when I leave the office.'
- 'I feel guilty when I'm on holiday . . . and I know I'm guilty of not taking enough time off.'
- 'I wake up guilty knowing that there are emails waiting for me on my Blackberry . . . '

Guilt shows up everywhere. When we're working, when we're not working. When we show up, when we switch off. When we bring work home and when we leave work undone. When we miss out on school plays, sports days and bedtimes, as well as when we take time off for our children, for sick days and school strikes. When we forget birthdays and miss deadlines, but also when we can't forget about work.

And its constant message is this: 'You don't have enough time. You're not doing enough.' Some of us even use guilt to spur us on, to tell ourselves and others: 'You have to do more.'

But what does guilt actually do?

Guilt distracts you

Ever notice how the thing you feel guilty about is never the thing you're focused on? When you're working, guilt tells you you're neglecting your family, your health, your house or your relationships. When you're not working, guilt taps you on the shoulder and reminds you of the email you forgot to send or the meeting you're not preparing for.

Guilt thrives on counting losses. All the things you've missed, not done or not doing right now. Forget the lovely Sunday afternoon you've just had with your kids and count the seconds you're not spending with them. Forget the magical moment you just had when he took off on his bike without you holding on, and keep beating yourself up about the first step you missed when you were at work. Forget the brilliant victory you've just pulled out of the bag at work, and keep counting the jobs that are still on your to-do list.

By default, guilt distracts and diminishes your capacity. Like trying to drive in one direction while looking in another or when a child starts running one way while looking somewhere else, it's exhausting, ineffective and frankly a disaster waiting to happen. You can't pay full attention to something if you're constantly looking over your shoulder, and guilt always draws your attention to what you're not doing.

Guilt devalues your time

Research from Stanford University Graduate School of Business suggests that people who are time affluent, who feel like they have more time, are people who regularly experience a sense of awe, being captivated by the present moment.[5]

Guilt on the other hand, steals your ability to be in the present. Instead of enjoying the time that you do have, you end up worrying about what you don't have time for, what's not been done and what's not gone well. Instead of giving yourself permission to be completely absorbed in the moment, to fully experience what's right in front of you, guilt whisks us away – your body might be present, but your mind starts time travelling – replaying past regrets and fretting about the future.

Worrying itself takes time, energy and attention. As cricketer Glenn Turner put it, 'Worrying is like a rocking chair, it gives you something to do, but it gets you nowhere.' The more you worry about not having enough time, the less time you seem to have.

Guilt disables you

What have you told yourself you'd love to do someday, when you have time? What do you find yourself saying you'd love to do 'if only you had the time'? What do you keep putting off, waiting for that elusive moment when everything else is done and you finally 'have time'?

Guilt holds you back from pursuing the things that really matter to you – that bold business idea or brave career move, the trip you've always wanted to make or the book you keep meaning to write. The stuff that matters to you, that perhaps nobody else is ever going to chase you up on.

If you took the rocking chair test, imagine yourself aged 96, looking back on your life, what would you be most proud of? What would you consider to have been time well spent? Chances are those are precisely the things that guilt tells you you don't have time for.

Not enough time

Guilt has a way of sneaking in and making itself at home. Somewhere along the line, we've accepted guilt as a permanent resident in our lives – sitting on our shoulder, at the dinner table, in the bath with our kids . . . and its constant message is 'not enough'. There's not enough time. You're not doing enough. You're not enough. The guilt-driven life is one of fear, where nothing is ever enough.

Guilt has you believing that you don't have enough time, but what if guilt is the very thing that's stealing your time? What if you stopped feeling guilty about your time? What if you said no to guilt?

What if you said ENOUGH?

Enough with the guilt trip. Enough with the exhausting cycle of never having, doing or being enough. Because quite frankly, that's not working. Let's redefine your relationship with time. Let's start a new conversation about time. Let's ditch the guilt, and start telling the truth about time.

Guilt tells you there's never enough. So let's start with enough. Instead of what you don't have time for, let's start talking about what you do have time for. Start with what you *do* have and what you *are* doing. Celebrate that and start from there.

When you start from enough, you stop getting distracted by trying to find more, and you make the most of what you do have. How much time do you have: ten minutes, ten days, ten months? Instead of wishing you had more, focus on what you do have and what you're going to do with it.

When you start from enough you appreciate what you have, you value it, love it, treasure it, enjoy it, instead of worrying about where the next thing's going to come from. Not sure how everything's going to play out next week? That's OK, you'll work it out. But if now's not the moment to figure it out, then let it go. Focus on the person, the moment, or the forkful of food that's right in front of you right now, and enjoy it.

When you start from enough you stop holding yourself back, and you actually start. And you know that's where the magic happens. It's from a place of enough that we grow and create more.

brilliant tip

Let's start with this: You have enough. You do enough. You are enough. Now what are you going to do with that?

How to feel like you have more time

Starting from enough also happens to be a great place to build more. Most productivity conversations start with 'not enough time', but in 2012 psychological scientists Melanie Rudd, Jennifer Aaker and Kathleen Vohs embarked on a study to understand: What makes people feel like they have more time? What makes some people time-rich, when others feel time-poor?[6]

They studied awe – the experience of being captivated by the present moment: 'Whether it's the breathtaking scope of the Grand Canyon, the ethereal beauty of the aurora borealis, or the exhilarating view from the top of the Eiffel Tower – at some point in our lives we've all had the feeling of being in a complete and overwhelming sense of awe.'[7]

They found that awe changes our subjective experience of time. It makes time slow down – not the actual ticking of the seconds, but in how we experience it. It expands our perception of time.

'When you feel awe, you feel very present – it captivates you in the current moment,' says Rudd. 'And when you are so focused on the here and now, the present moment is expanded – and time along with it.'[8]

This certainly chimes with Gay Hendrick's theory of Einstein Time (time is relative) versus Newtonian Time (time is finite) in his book *The Big Leap*.[9] Time is relative: an hour with your beloved feels like a minute; a minute on a hot stove feels like an hour. Depending on what we do, space seems to narrow or to expand, time seems to slow down or accelerate.

As one Head of Talent put it: 'I work 8 to 5 with half an hour for lunch and because it's my bliss it feels like about two hours. Time is weird.'

Awe also makes us feel like we have more time available. We become more patient and less materialistic, and more willing to volunteer our time to help other people. People who feel like they have more time are more generous with their time, and experience greater life satisfaction too:

Experiences of awe bring people into the present moment, and being in the present moment underlies awe's capacity to adjust time perception, influence decisions, and make life feel more satisfying than it would otherwise.[10]

Magic moments

How easy is it to generate awe? Do you have to travel to the Grand Canyon or Paris? Or might these moments be found a bit closer to home too?

Perhaps it's the feeling of being beautifully overwhelmed by a sunset or a stranger's generosity. Or being completely lost in a book, a work of art or a hot bubble bath. Or those goosebump moments when life surprises and delights you.

 **action**

Here's an experiment – start noticing your magic moments and let yourself be captivated by them. Then capture them – write it down or tell someone else. I have one client who has cultivated a habit of capturing his AMGLs: Achievements, Magic Moments, Gratitudes and Learning Moments – writing them in a notebook roughly once a month, and now has five years' worth of these to look back on.

What might your moments of awe be? Whatever it is, when we allow ourselves to be captivated by the present moment, we'll feel like we have all the time in the world.

What are your feelings trying to tell you?

Feelings of stress, guilt and overwhelm can be a sign that something is out of kilter with your values, beliefs or expectations. Sometimes those expectations are wildly unrealistic (I must be all things to all people and get everything right) and lead to the constant guilt that just makes you feel rubbish, but sometimes your feelings can serve you if it helps you to put a finger on something specific you want to change or do differently.

 **action**

1   Check your feelings. What's behind this feeling? What thoughts, worries, or fears are creating this feeling of guilt, stress, frustration or overwhelm? What are you believing to be true about this situation?

2   Challenge your thinking. Ask yourself: 'How true is that, really?'
     How true is that underlying belief that emails need to be answered
     immediately, or that your boss is out to get you, or that every moment
     you're not with your kids you're neglecting them? Sometimes your
     feelings can come from underlying beliefs that are based on past truths,
     part truths or pure imagination.

3   Clarify what's important. Rather than focusing on the fear or worry
     itself, what is it that you value that feels threatened here? Get to the
     core of what's important, so you can focus on making changes that
     honour what you do want, rather than react to what you don't want.

4   Change your perspective. What's another way to look at this? What are
     the positives? What else is going on or going well? Do you see a heavy
     schedule, or a week full of opportunities? Pressure to perform, or the
     opportunity to do your best work? Curveballs or plot twists? Failure or
     the opportunity to do something new? Perspective matters. What you
     see shapes your world and how you live in it.

5   Choose your response: What can you do differently? What positive
     changes can you make? What actions can you take that will help you
     to honour what's important?

---

brilliant recap

Overwhelm, stress and guilt can be common feelings in today's
world of work, and if left unchecked can steal our focus, energy and
ability to do our best work. When we check and challenge these
feelings, when we choose to see things from a different perspective,
we can stop fighting time, and enjoying more of it. We can prime
ourselves to do our best work, and focus our energy on what
matters.

References

[1] Allen, D., 2015. *Getting Things Done: The Art of Stress-free Productivity*. Piatkus: London.

[2] Covey, S.R., 2005. *The 7 Habits of Highly Effective People: Powerful Lessons in Personal Change*. Simon & Schuster: London.

[3] Dr Rob Archer, The Career Psychologist. Available at: www.thecareerpsychologist.com

[4] McGonigal, K., 2013. 'How to make stress your friend', TED Global. Available at: www.ted.com/talks/kelly_mcgonigal_how_to_make_stress_your_friend?language=en

[5] Rudd, M., Vohs, K. D. and Aaker, J., 2012. 'Awe expands people's perception of time, alters decision making, and enhances well-being', *Psychological Science* 23(10).

[6] Ibid.

[7] Ibid.

[8] Greenberg, S., 2012. 'Jennifer Aaker: How to feel like you have more time', Stanford Business. Available at: www.gsb.stanford.edu/insights/jennifer-aaker-how-feel-you-have-more-time

[9] Hendrick, G., 2009. *The Big Leap*. HarperCollins (Kindle edition): London.

[10] Rudd, M., Vohs, K. D. and Aaker, J., 2012. 'Awe expands people's perception of time, alters decision making, and enhances well-being', *Psychological Science* 23(10).

CHAPTER 10

How productive are you now?

f you've been putting this book into action as you go along, this is your opportunity to reflect on your journey so far. If you've raced ahead, nodding away thinking 'that's a good idea!' and 'I'd like to give this a go', this is your opportunity to put your action plan together.

Because none of this works if you don't work it. It's up to you to put it into action, to bring it to life in your working life. Adapt and tailor the strategies to suit you, and as you do, notice the difference, track your progress and build on what works.

A quick temperature check

Take a look at the checklist below. Put a tick next to those you feel you can comfortably say yes to already. Put a star next to those you need to work on and have an action plan in place, and a question mark for the areas where you'd like to give some more consideration, and perhaps revisit the chapters.

I feel in control of my workflow.	
I have a system in place that captures the incoming and leaves my brain free to focus.	
I regularly practise celebrating success.	
I have ways of managing my working environment to suit me.	
I am aware of my mind monkeys and recognise their tactics.	

▶

I can bypass procrastination with play and sidestep resistance with Baby Steps.	
I am regularly eating my frogs!	
I am having better conversations with my mind monkeys.	
I regularly use impact thinking to evaluate what's worth doing, and what's not worth doing.	
I measure, celebrate and encourage results over busy.	
I am mindful of fake work and use place power moves to remove the temptation.	
I make space for real work.	
I employ stealth and camouflage tactics and proactively manage my availability and attention.	
I have productive conversations with my team and my boss, so that we can work well together.	
I take a professional approach to firefighting.	
I recognise the importance of margin and am regularly taking opportunities to build it in.	
I have clear boundaries that communicate what I value.	
I actively take a lead in establishing how I serve, work and give my best.	
I am more interested in failing well than hiding mistakes or apportioning blame.	
I practise saying no.	
I understand my personal motivators, frustrations, natural strengths and fears.	
I adapt my personal productivity strategies to suit my personality.	
I am aware of my strengths, when they are overused or hidden, and how to harness them.	
I clearly communicate my needs to my colleagues, and understand their needs too.	
I have a daily rhythm that harnesses my best energy and creates momentum for my work to flow.	

I create my own finish lines and switch off on a regular, sustainable basis.	
I have a wobbly line and I honour my basic human needs.	
I understand that my productivity depends on life outside of work as well as life at work.	
I can identify when I am experiencing overwhelm, and use practical techniques to navigate through this.	
I have a healthy relationship with stress.	
I no longer feel guilty about what I'm not doing.	
I take my time to notice magic moments and experience awe, and as a result, I have more time.	

Your action plan

The quickest way to send yourself into overwhelm, would be to commit to do everything all at once. Remember that Baby Steps move mountains: extraordinary results come from taking ordinary steps every day in the right direction.

So choose your first action, and make that happen. Then come back when you're ready for more. As we set out at the beginning of this book, productivity is always a work in progress. Don't buy into the perfection myth, that everything has to be flawless or organised within an inch of its life. Focus on the next step, and celebrate progress, not perfection.

Do make this your own. Use the thoughts, tools and tips in this book to enable and inspire your own thinking. Experiment with what works for you, and above all, have fun using it, because after all, that's what brilliant productivity is ultimately about – doing your best work, having fun doing it, and enjoying life at work and life outside of work.

brilliant action

My Brilliant Productivity Plan:

What I'm going to work on first is:

....

And here's what I'm going to do to make it happen:

● in the next six days

....

....

....

● in the next six weeks

....

....

....

● in the next six months

....

....

....

Final thoughts

'Not enough time, too much to do' is how most of our productivity conversations start.

But when we look deeper, we find that time is not the enemy. The more we fight time, the less of it we have. If you feel like time is always running away from you, that you never seem to have enough time. If you are constantly busy, rushing round after other people, wondering when you'll ever have some time to yourself. If you're waiting for when you have more time . . .

Here are three words for you: Take Your Time.

Here's why:

When we don't have enough time we rush. When my daughter tries to wriggle her foot into her snug winter boots without losing her balance, and my son tugs and fiddles with his laces, I find myself saying, 'It's OK, take your time'. Because if they rush, it gets harder, and more frustrating, and takes longer.

When we don't have enough time we hold back or give up. What have you told yourself you'll do when you have time? What would you love to do if only you had the time? Rest, sleep, me time, read a book, write a book, take a holiday, go for a walk, upgrade the software, expand the business, take the risk, train, delegate, think, plan, prepare, go for a run, be still . . . So often the things we put off are the things that would add meaning, simplicity or joy to our lives. The things that make life better, and time worthwhile.

So many people wait. They wait for the work to finish, the demands to stop, the constant busyness to slow down, so they can finally have time to do what they want to do. And yet, that time never comes, because the work never stops and there's always more to do.

When we don't have enough time we faff, we procrastinate, we look for distraction. Something to scratch the itch, to quell the sound of the clock ticking, to make us feel like we're doing *something*. Yet often when we just sit with it, take our time, for what might seem like forever, but in reality is probably just 20 minutes, the momentum starts flowing, and we get it done.

When we don't have enough time, we can miss the moments. As the saying goes, life is not measured by the number of breaths we take, but by the moments that take our breath away. But when we obsess over counting the seconds, we can miss the moments. Moments of profound joy and intense silliness, roaring laughter and peaceful silence, heartwarming connection and satisfying rest. Whether it's the simple pleasures or crazy adventures. These are the moments that make life worth living. These are the moments to take our time over.

The truth is, we have time – and we choose how we spend it.

As one workshop delegate put it, 'If I choose to look at my work email at the weekend, and see something that upsets me, I'm the one who has chosen to let email ruin my weekend. It's my choice, not anybody else's.' The uncomfortable truth is, if you never seem to have any time for yourself, your agenda and what matters to you, you're choosing not to give any time to yourself.

We make that choice, by what we say yes and no to, what we commit to and what we fail to commit to, what we make ourselves available to, and what we pay attention to. It's our time, to use or to give away, as we choose. And the beauty is, when we stop seeing time as something that runs away without us, when we start taking our time, we choose how we experience that time.

We can't change time, but we can change our experience of it. Sometimes time flies, sometimes it drags, and that's nothing to do with the seconds, minutes and hours, but everything to do with what we choose. So here's what I propose. Let's stop talking about time like there's not enough, like it's some unstoppable tsunami that we're trying to wrestle into submission.

Let's just take our time.

If you feel like life is doing you, rather than the other way round, take your time. It's yours, to do as you choose. You are in control. You really are.

If you've been waiting for the perfect time, that never seems to come, I want to say to you: Take your time. It's yours. Take it, run with it, play with it, live it.

If you're dealing with new ground, ill health or challenging circumstances that mean you're not going as fast as you'd like, it's OK. You're doing great. Give yourself the space. Be patient, be kind. Take your time. You'll get there.

And if you're taking time off, take it, savour it, enjoy every moment. Don't count it by seconds, measure it by moments. Enjoy every moment.

Whatever your circumstances, whatever lies before you, here's my challenge, and my invitation.

Take Your Time.

What did you think of this book?

We're really keen to hear from you about this book, so that we can make our publishing even better.

Please log on to the following website and leave us your feedback.

It will only take a few minutes and your thoughts are invaluable to us.

www.pearsoned.co.uk/bookfeedback

Index